If language is not correct,
then what is said is not what is meant;
if what is said is not what is meant,
then what ought to be done remains undone.
                                    —Confucius

Writing that <u>works</u>

Previous books

How to Advertise
by Kenneth Roman and Jane Maas

The Unpublished David Ogilvy
Edited by Joel Raphaelson

Writing
that <u>works</u>

How to improve your memos,
letters, reports, speeches, resumes,
plans, and other business papers

Second edition, revised, enlarged,
and updated

Kenneth Roman
and Joel Raphaelson

HarperPerennial
A Division of HarperCollinsPublishers

HarperCollins books may be purchased for educational, business, or sales promotional use. For information, please call or write: Special Markets Department, HarperCollins Publishers, Inc., 10 East 53rd Street, New York, NY 10022. Telephone: (212) 207-7528; Fax: (212) 207-7222.

FIRST EDITION

Designed by Marcia Sawa

Library of Congress Cataloging-in-Publication Data

Roman, Kenneth.
    Writing that works / by Ken Roman and Joel Raphaelson.—2nd ed., rev., enl., and updated.
        p. cm.
    ISBN 0-06-271550-X (cloth)
    ISBN 0-06-273144-0 (pbk.)
    1. English language—Business English.   2. English language—Rhetoric.   3. Business writing.   I. Raphaelson, Joel.   II. Title.
PE1479.B87R65   1992
808'.066651—dc20   91-58285

92 93 94 95 96 CC/MB 10 9 8 7 6 5 4 3 2
    93 94 95 MPC 10 9 8 7 6 5 4 3   (pbk.)

Contents

Preface

A Practical Handbook— Expanded and Updated

When this book first came out, nobody we knew had a word processor or a personal computer. Nobody we knew got faxes or electronic mail. That was only ten years ago. Never before has the technology of writing and the way we communicate in business undergone so great a change so fast.

We wrote the book originally to help those millions of nonprofessional writers who must use the written word to get results—in business, in government, in education, in the arts. That remains its purpose.

But the pace of change has led us to take a fresh look at how the old principles apply in today's conditions. The personal computer and the word processor have entered both home and workplace to such a degree that we added a chapter on how they can help you improve everything you write. And we have revised a number of other chapters to take their pervasive influence into account.

This edition takes note of the new terms that the new technologies have launched into common use. We welcome those that say something more simply and directly than was previously possible—"input" and "output," for example. We deplore lingo that replaces simple and direct words with techno-jargon, and we wag our fingers at some frequent offenders.

We added a chapter on proposals and recommendations, an important facet of business writing that we unaccountably overlooked in the first edition.

And our consciousness has been raised to the pitfalls of sexist language. Avoiding sexist terms doesn't mean barbarizing the language in order to please extremists. "Herstory" in place of history, "womyn" to avoid "wo<u>men</u>" and "s/he" strike us as having no place in grown-up circles. We think there is plenty of point, however, in minimizing gender-specific language when referring to both men and women. Offended readers are unlikely to be sympathetic to your message.

Finally, we have freshened our examples and sharpened our points by practicing what we preach about editing.

Nothing in this book is academic or theoretical. You will find little about grammar, even though good grammar is essential to good writing.

You will find advice you can *act* on, whenever you have to convert blank paper into a letter, a memorandum, a report, a recommendation, a proposal, a speech, a resume. You'll get help from specific side-by-side examples of good writing versus bad.

You don't need talent to be able to write effectively. For sure, writing is hard work even for the best writers (and even on a word processor), but the *principles* of good writing are simple. They are easy to understand and easy to put into use. Our purpose is to help you say what you want to say, with less difficulty and more confidence, and get the results you're looking for from everything you write.

1

People Who Write Well Do Well

ë

American executives spend a fifth of their working hours writing. But they don't think they're much good at it. More precisely, they rate a third of all the business material they have to read as "unclear, poorly written, or confusing."

So says a 1990 survey of vice presidents of 200 of the nation's most prominent companies. The survey doesn't say, but we suppose that many of the unhappy VPs are perpetrators as well as victims, confusers as well as confusees.

Things aren't any better in the academic world. In the fall of 1991, the commissioner of New York State's Department of Education ordered his 250 highest-ranking officials to take a 3½-hour class in writing. According to *The New York Times,* the commissioner had grown "frustrated that too many of the letters and memos passing through his office were 'confusing' and 'did not answer questions quickly enough or directly enough.' "

We could fill a dozen pages with complaints of this sort. They add up to a chorus of laments that so few people can write well—that so few can put a thought on paper in words that make it clear, state it precisely, and take no more of the reader's time than the subject calls for.

When you write a letter or a report or a plan, you want something to happen. You may want your reader to:

- Understand your report and endorse your conclusions
- Approve your plan—and pay for it
- Send money for your charity, your candidate, your product, your service
- Invite you to a job interview
- Know exactly what to do next—and when to do it

You are not likely to achieve the results you seek if your writing is murky, long-winded, bogged down by imprecisions or jargon, and topsy-turvy in its order of thought.

Your reader does not have much time. If you want to hold the attention of busy people, your writing must cut through to the heart of the matter. It must require a minimum of time and effort on the reader's part.

The importance of this increases with the importance of your reader. At any level, readers are likely to be swamped with paperwork. Junior executives may feel obliged to plow through everything that comes across the desk. The president doesn't—and damned well won't.

A senior executive says this about a client:

His desk is usually absolutely clean, but I know that some-where in that man's life there's a tremendous pile of paper. If I want him to read the memo himself, I'd better get right to the point and I'd better be clear, or he'll just pass it along to somebody else, with a testy little note asking for a translation.

The better you write, the less time your boss must spend rewriting your stuff. If you are ambitious, it won't hurt to make life easier for people above you. Bad writing slows things down; good writing speeds them up.

People act on matters that have been put forward clearly and coherently. Write well and you'll get more done.

The only way some people know you is through your writing. It can be your most frequent point of contact, or your *only* one, with people important to your career—major customers, senior clients, your own top management.

To those women and men, your writing is you. It reveals how your mind works. Is it forceful or fatuous, deft or clumsy, crisp or soggy? Readers who don't know you judge you from the evidence in your writing.

It is best to stick to standard English usage and to observe the rules of spelling and punctuation. We advise this not out of academic fussiness but from observing how things are. If you write "it's" with an apostrophe to signify the possessive of "it" (wrong), instead of the contraction of "it is" (right), not all readers will detect your lapse. But those who do may be the ones who count. For better or worse, there still seems to be some correlation between literacy and seniority.

Observant people will note your taste in language as sharply as they take measure of your taste in clothes or your manners. They cannot help forming an impression of you from what they see of you. A large part of what they see may be what you put on paper.

Important issues are usually examined in writing, either in a formal paper or a presentation. It isn't enough that you know all about your subject. You must make yourself clear to somebody who has only a fraction of your expertise. Above all, you must express your point of view persuasively. As old hands in the advertising business, we have seen hundreds of papers that assert an enthusiastic point of view, but astonishingly few that make a persuasive case. Most of the time the case itself is a good one. But the writer self-destructs in any or all of the ways we go into later on.

Your ability to write persuasively can help you to get done what you want and to arrive at your goal—today, this month, or during the decades of your career.

The former head of ITT, Harold Geneen, said: "It is an immutable law of business that words are words, promises are promises, but only performance is reality."

By itself, good writing is no guarantee of success. But words are more than words, and business writing does not exist in a vacuum. What you write will always have a purpose and if you write well you are more likely to achieve it, and to succeed.

2

Don't Mumble— and Other Principles of Effective Writing

&

Most people "write badly because they cannot think clearly," observed H. L. Mencken. The reason they cannot think clearly, he went on, is that "they lack the brains."

It follows that if you *can* think clearly, you have a fighting chance of being able to write well. But clear thinking is only the first step. The suggestions in this chapter go on from there. They will help you to put on paper exactly what you have in mind.

"I don't know what makes business writing so dull," somebody said, "but whatever it is, it works." None of our suggestions are aimed specifically at making your writing more interesting, but all of them will tend to have that effect. This is because dullness isn't the root of the problem.

To the extent that you find your work interesting,

it should only be natural to find interesting anything you read in connection with it. What readers sum up vaguely as "dull" results from a mixture of other, more specific flaws. Lack of clarity, verbosity, and mumbling are high among them. Therefore:

1. Don't mumble

Once you've decided what you want to say, come right out and say it. Mumblers command less attention than people who speak up.

Keep in mind E. B. White's sobering injunction: "When you say something, make sure you have said it. The chances of your having said it are only fair."

Instead of this . . .	This
It is generally desirable to communicate your thoughts in a forthright manner. Toning your point down and tiptoeing around it may, in many circumstances, tempt the reader to tune out and allow his mind to wander.	Don't mumble.

2. Make the organization of your writing clear

When you write anything longer than a few paragraphs, start by telling the reader where you are going. Like:

This paper proposes that the company invest $1,000,000 in a library.

First you must know where you are going yourself. Make an outline of your major points. Place supporting details in their proper position. Then, in your paper, use your outline to signal the major points for your reader. Underline and number each important section heading. This serves the same purpose as chapter titles in a book.

End with a summary. And keep in mind that a *summary* is not a *conclusion*. Your summary should introduce no new ideas; it should summarize, as briefly as possible, the most important points you have made.

If your paper comes to a conclusion, your summary should summarize that, too. The purpose of a summary is to fix the essentials of your message in your reader's mind.

> Summary: *Make an outline; use your outline to help your reader; number and underline section headings; summarize.*

3. Use short paragraphs, short sentences— and short words

Six articles start at the top of the front page of every issue of *The Wall Street Journal.* The first paragraphs of these articles are never more than three sentences long. More than half the paragraphs contain only a single sentence.

The first sentences themselves are crisp and compact:

> *It all began to crumble the afternoon Mom's Best Cookies Inc. fired Mom.*

> *Dying young fostered the cult of James Dean, and it hasn't hurt his hometown any.*

> *It's official—Wall Street is declaring war on sexism.*

By contrast, here is an example of the kind of mumbling first sentence that confronts people in their office reading:

This provides the Argus, Mitchell & Dohn perspective on a consumers'-eye view of the current position and growth potential of Blake's Tea and Jones's Tea, the major entries of National Beverages in the English tea market.

The Wall Street Journal now sells more copies than any other daily in America. Readers and editors alike give much of the credit to its readability.

Journal editors have put into practice this simple principle: Short sentences and short paragraphs are easier to read than long ones. And easier to understand.

As for short *words,* don't turn your back on the riches and subtleties of the English language. Nobody will excoriate you for using a long word whose precise meaning no shorter word duplicates.

But you should always prefer the short word to the long one that means the same thing:

Use this	**Not this**
Now	Currently
Start	Initiate
Show	Indicate
Finish	Finalize
Speed up, move along	Expedite
Use	Utilize
Place, put	Position

4. Make your writing active—and personal

Good writers choose the active voice over the passive voice whenever possible—and it's possible in most instances. Active verbs add energy to your writing. That's why they're called *active.*

This simple measure also improves your writing by making it more personal, a human being talking rather than an institution. The passive voice hides who is speaking or taking action; the active voice reveals it.

Passive, impersonal	Active, personal
It is recommended	We recommend
He should be told	Please tell him
Personal sacrifices are being made, although the degree of participation is not absolutely identifiable.	We see people making sacrifices. How many people? We can't say for sure.

A lot of business writings mumble along in the passive voice because high school English teachers told us not to start sentences with "I." If that worries you, you can still find good ways to substitute active for passive verbs.

Here is a typical passive construction—followed by examples of active alternatives.

It is respectfully requested that you send a representative to our conference.

All of us here hope that you'll send a representative.
Won't you please send a representative . . .
Somebody representing your company would add a lot . . .
Will you give serious thought to sending a representative?
You can see how much a representative from your company would contribute . . .
Without a representative from your company, our conference would be a fizzle.

You might protest that these alternatives don't all say quite the same thing. Exactly! Yet another advantage of the active voice is that it tends to push you to decide exactly what you want to say, to be more specific.

5. Avoid vague modifiers

A memo complains that a certain outcome "was reasonably unexpected." Not only passive, but ambiguous and vague. Just how unexpected was the outcome? Or does the writer mean that a reasonable person would not have expected it at all? Depending on the intention, the memo might have said:

Few of us expected this outcome.

OR

Although I didn't expect this outcome, it wasn't a complete surprise.

State your meaning precisely:

Vague	Precise
Very overspent	Overspent by $10,000
Slightly behind schedule	One day late

Don't listen to anybody who tells you to weed out adjectives and adverbs as a matter of principle. They are parts of speech, often indispensable to precise expression. Distinguish between *lazy* adjectives and adverbs and *vigorous* ones. The lazy ones are so overused in some contexts that they have become clichés:

Very good	*Great* success
Awfully nice	*Richly* deserved
Basically accurate	*Vitally* important

By contrast, vigorous adjectives and adverbs sharpen your point:

Instantly accepted	*Tiny* raise
Rudely turned down	*Moist* handshake
Short meeting	*Tiresome* speech
Crisp presentation	*Black* coffee
Baffling instructions	*Lucid* recommendation

Choose adjectives and adverbs that make your meaning more precise. Do not use them as mere exclamation points.

6. Use down-to-earth language

Avoid technical jargon. There is always a simple, down-to-earth word that says the same thing as the show-off fad word or vague abstraction. As we write, a leading offender is "proactive"—supposedly indicating the opposite of "reactive." Try "active" (the real word) or, for more emphasis, "take the initiative."

A recent entry is "off-line," as in "Let's go off-line on that subject." What they're trying to say is, "Let's discuss that separately, outside the meeting." Then there's "re-engineering"—in contexts that have nothing to do with engineers. Anything that's changed in any way is likely to be described as "re-engineered." We might even have said, without raising eyebrows in trendy circles, that we had "re-engineered" this book. What we did say—that we had expanded the book and updated it—may stir you less but tells you more.

A major television network fills five-second gaps here and there with odd bits of information that it calls "factoids." We don't know what's wrong with "odd facts," a down-to-earth expression that everybody understands, but we do know that whoever rolled out "factoid" didn't bother to look it up. It means "a statement that's fictitious or unsubstantiated"—in other words, not a fact.

Here are some other examples of showing off—and the down-to-earth alternatives:

Jargon	Down-to-earth English
Implement	Carry out
Viable	Practical, workable
Interface	Discuss, meet, work with
Optimum	Best, largest possible
To impact	To affect, to do to
Resultful	Effective, achieve results
Meaningful	Real, actual, tangible
Judgmentally	I think
Net net	Conclusion
Suboptimal	Less than ideal
Bottom line	Final result
Push the envelope	Test the limits
Scope down (from *microscope*)	Look at more closely
Scope out (from *telescope*)	Take a long view

NOTE: Popular usage has confused *parameters* with *perimeter.* If you mean limits, say *limits.*

What's wrong with jargon becomes obvious when words like these come at you in clusters, which is how they tend to arrive:

Jargon	Down-to-earth English
It is believed that with the parameters that have been imposed by your management, a viable program may be hard to evolve. Net net: If our program is to impact the consumer to the optimum, meaningful interface with your management may be necessitated.	We believe that the limits your management set may rule out an effective program. If we expect to reach our goal, we'd better ask your management to listen to our case.

The kind of writing on the left is long-winded and heavy-handed. It is what E. B. White calls "the language of mutilation"—it mutilates your meaning.

The language on the right is clear and direct. It illuminates your meaning.

7. Be specific

One of the main weaknesses in much business writing is the overuse of generalities. The writer has something specific in mind, but doesn't put it down on paper. The reader is left to guess. Friendly readers may guess sympathetically, but if you're neutral or skeptical, you will remain uninformed and unimpressed.

The first draft of a letter reporting on a series of educational seminars in Wyoming said:

> *Our adult program was a great success. We attracted more students from more places than ever before.*

The reader, not knowing whether the increase in students was one or a hundred and lacking any other specific information, must take the generalized claim of success on faith. When rewritten, the letter said:

> *Our enrollment doubled to 560. Students came from Wyoming and 27 other states, and from Germany and Canada.*

There can now be no doubt about the success of the program. The specifics speak for themselves.

8. Choose the right word

Know the precise meaning of every word you use. Here are some words that many people confuse:

To **affect** something is to have an influence on it: *The new program affects only the clerical staff.*

Effect can mean a result (noun) or to bring about (verb): *The effect of the new program on the morale of the drivers will be zero; it effects no change outside the clerical staff.*

It's is the contraction of "it is." *It's vital that profits keep growing.*

Its is the possessive form of "it." No apostrophe. *Its profits grow year after year.*

Principal is the first in rank or importance: *Our principal problem is lack of cash flow.*

Principle is a guiding rule: *Our principle is to use our own money rather than to borrow.*

Imply means to suggest indirectly: *Her report implies that she will soon promote her assistant.*

Infer means to draw meaning out of something: *The assistant infers from her report that he will soon be promoted.*

i.e. *(id est)* means "that is": *He preferred short names; i.e., nothing longer than four letters.*

e.g. *(exempli gratia)* means "for example": *He gave all his products short names; e.g., Hit, Miss, Duck, Dive.*

Mitigate means to lessen in force or intensity: *She mitigated the bad news by giving everybody the afternoon off.*

Militate means to have force as evidence usually in a case *against* something: *The bad news militates against an early end to the raise freeze.*

Gratuitous means unasked for, excessive: *He had done his job to perfection for years. The advice from the newcomer was gratuitous.*

Grateful, gratitude. You know what these words mean. The point here is that they have no connection with *gratuitous.*

Appraise means to measure, to assess the value or nature of something: *The general appraised the enemy's strength before ordering the attack.*

Apprise means to inform in detail: *The chief of staff apprised the colonels of the general's appraisal of the situation.*

Fortuitous means happening by chance, accidental. *Being seated next to his ex-wife was fortuitous—and unfortunate.*

Fortunate means favored by good fortune—lucky.

Alternate (verb) means to go back and forth from one to another: *The coach alternated between passing plays and running plays.* As noun or adjective, it carries the same sense: *Mike and Jim are the coach's alternates; they play on alternate sets of downs.*

Alternative refers to a choice among two or more possibilities: *The coach faced the alternatives—go for the first down and possible victory, or punt to preserve the tie.*

Definite is most often used to mean positive, absolutely certain: *It is now definite that the factory will open on schedule.*

Definitive means complete and authoritative, determining once and for all: *It was the definitive design for a steel mill, a model for all others.*

Indifferent means that you don't care how it comes out: *The chairman, recognizing the triviality of the proposal, was indifferent.*

Disinterested is not the same as "uninterested." It means neutral and objective: *Amid the passions raging on both sides, only the chairman, recognizing the importance of the decision, managed to remain disinterested.*

Fulsome means excessive to the point of insincerity: *His fulsome praise was a transparent attempt at flattery.*

Full, abundant are in no way synonymous with fulsome. They carry their own familiar meanings.

15

Notable means worthy of note: *His research on Jack the Ripper is notable for its thoroughness.*

Notorious means famous in an unsavory way: *Jack the Ripper was perhaps the most notorious criminal of the nineteenth century.*

Into must be handled with caution. The headline writer wrote, MURDER SUSPECTS TURN THEMSELVES INTO POLICE—stunning as magic, but not what he meant. When the preposition *in* belongs to the verb—"to turn oneself in"—you can't use *into*.

In to is not synonymous with *into*. You go *into* the house, or you go *in to find* your wallet. You look *into* the subject before you *hand your paper in to* your boss. The rules are too complicated to help. Be alert to the difference and use your ear.

When you confuse words like these, your reader may conclude that you don't know any better. Illiteracy does not breed respect.

9. Make it perfect

No typos, no misspellings, no errors in numbers or dates. If your writing is slipshod in any of these ways, however minor they may seem to you, your reader may reasonably question how much care and thought you have put into it.

Spelling is a special problem. Good spellers are an intolerant lot, and your reader could be among them. Whenever you are in doubt about how a word is spelled, look it up in the dictionary.

If you are an incurably bad speller, make sure your drafts get checked by someone who isn't thus handicapped.

10. Come to the point

Churchill could have mumbled that "the situation in regard to France is very serious." What he did say was, "The news from France is bad."

Take the time to boil down what you want to say, and express it confidently in simple, declarative sentences. Remember the man who apologized for writing such a long letter, explaining that he didn't have time to write a short one.

There are only 266 words in the Gettysburg Address. The shortest sentence in the New Testament may be the most moving: "Jesus wept."

11. Write simply and naturally— the way you talk

Some of this book, as with much business writing, was drafted or edited on an airplane. There is a mysterious person somewhere who writes the scripts for all flight attendants, someone who writes "Please extinguish all smoking materials" instead of "Please put out your cigarettes." Or, "The pilot has illuminated the seat belt sign, indicating our initial approach into the Houston area." Is the pilot really going to take a first try at landing somewhere near Houston? Who is writing this stuff?

Most Americans are taught that the written language and the spoken language are entirely different. They learn to write in a stiff style and to steer clear of anything that sounds natural and colloquial.

Stiff	Natural
The reasons are fourfold	There are four reasons
Importantly	The important point is
Visitation	Visit

Notice how often somebody will say "It sounds just like her" in praise of some particularly effective writing. What you write should sound just like you talking *when you're at your best*—when your ideas flow swiftly and in good order, when your syntax is smooth, your vocabulary accurate, and afterward you think that you couldn't possibly have put things any better than you did.

A first step in achieving that effect is to use only those words and phrases and sentences that you might actually *say* to your reader if you were face-to-face. If you wouldn't say it, if it doesn't *sound* like you, why write it?

The tone of your writing will vary as your readers vary. You would speak more formally to the President of the United States, meeting him for the first time, than to your Uncle Max. For the same reason, a letter to the President would naturally be more formal than a letter to a relative.

But it should still sound like you.

12. Strike out words you don't need

The song goes, "Softly, as in a morning sunrise"—and Ring Lardner explained that this was as opposed to a late afternoon or evening sunrise. Poetic license may be granted for a song, but not for expressions like these:

Don't write	Write
Advance plan	Plan
Take action	Act
Equally as	Equally
Hold a meeting	Meet
Study in depth	Study
New innovations	Innovations

Don't write	Write
Consensus of opinion	Consensus
At the present time, at this point in time	Now
Until such time as	Until
In the majority of instances	In most cases, usually
On a local basis	Locally
Basically unaware of	Did not know
The overall plan	The Plan
In the area of	Roughly
With regard to, in connection with	About
In view of, on the basis of	Because
In the event of	If
For the purpose of, in order to	To
Despite the fact that	Although

13. Use current standard English

A few years ago, a copywriter wrote this sentence in a draft of an advertisement to persuade more people to read *The New York Times:*

> *He always acted like he knew what he was talking about.*

Musing over the use of "like" in place of "as though" or "as if," someone at the *Times* said: "Yes, I guess that use of 'like' will become standard in five or ten years, but I don't think *The New York Times* should pioneer in these matters."

The pioneers have multiplied since this book first came out, but we'd advise you on principle to be among the last to join them. New usage offends many ears; established usage offends nobody. Had the copywriter written "He always acted as if he knew

19

what he was talking about," it would have seemed both natural and literate.

> *The old rule is simple: Don't use "like" in any case where "as if" or "as though" would fit comfortably.*

"Hopefully" is another word whose misuse still annoys many literate people. It is *not* synonymous with "I hope that." It means "in a hopeful manner" or "in a hopeful state of mind," as in:

> *I opened the envelope hopefully; perhaps it would contain the check I was waiting for.*

If you write "Hopefully, the check will be in the envelope," you are actually saying that the *check* will be sitting there in the envelope in an optimistic state of mind. What you mean is, "I hope the check will be in the envelope."

Nothing will call your literacy into question so promptly as using "I" for "me," or "she" for "her." Many people, though they have degrees from reputable colleges, make this illiterate mistake: "He asked both Helen and I to go to the convention." Try the pronoun alone. You would never write, "He asked I to go to the convention."

14. Don't write like a lawyer or a bureaucrat

Lawyers say that they have to write to each other in language like this:

> *BLANK Corporation, a corporation organized under the laws of the State of New South Wales, wishes to permit holders of its Ordinary Shares who are resident in or nationals of the United States, its territories or possessions ("U.S. Holders") to participate in the Dividend Reinvestment Plan (the "DRP") on essentially the same terms as those available to its other shareholders ("Non-U.S. Holders), and to provide the means by which holders of*

20

> *ADRs (as defined below) who are resident in or nationals of the United States, its territories or possessions ("U.S. Holders of ADRs") may indirectly participate, through the Depository, in the DRP. Toward this end, BLANK has adopted amendments to the DRP (as amended, the "Amended DRP") (a copy of which is attached hereto) to permit such participation.*

Somewhat defensively, lawyers explain that such language is essential to precision in contracts and such. Perhaps, but we suspect that the same ideas could be expressed more briefly, more clearly, and without any dangerous increase in ambiguity:

> *BLANK Corporation wants to offer holders of its Ordinary Shares who are U.S. citizens or residents the opportunity to participate in its Dividend Reinvestment Plan (DRP) on the same basis as non-U.S. holders. This includes U.S. holders of ADRs as well.*
>
> *BLANK has amended the DRP to enable this participation, and a copy of the amended DRP is attached.*

Whatever excuses lawyers may have, there are none for the business counterpart of this sort of writing, known as "bureaucratese." Its symptoms are long sentences, abbreviations, clauses within clauses, and a technical precision so elaborate that misunderstanding is unthinkable except that nobody can understand it in the first place.

If you find yourself writing like that, try putting down what you want to say the way you would say it to your reader if you were talking to him or her face-to-face. Don't worry if the result is too casual. Once you've got the main idea down in plain English, you'll find it easy to adjust the tone of voice.

One way to start breaking the habit of writing in bureaucratese or legalese is to banish from your writing unnecessary Latin. For example, "Re," meaning "in the matter of," is never necessary outside the most formal legal documents. You don't need it in headings or titles any more than the Bible needs "Re: Genesis."

15. Keep in mind what your reader doesn't know

Your reader seldom knows ahead of time where you are going or what you are trying to say. Never expect people to read your *mind* as well as your letter or paper.

Take into account how much you can assume your reader knows—what background information, what facts, what technical terms.

Watch your abbreviations. Will they be an indecipherable code to some readers? Might they be ambiguous even to those in the know?

> *M is code for a thousand in the United States, for a million in England; 9/12 means September 12 here—December 9 over there.*

If you must use abbreviations like M and MM, define them the first time they appear in your paper. "The cost per thousand (CPM) is a figure that we will keep an eye on throughout this proposal."

16. Punctuate carefully

Proper punctuation functions like road signs, helping your reader to navigate your sentences. A left-out comma, or a comma in the wrong place, can confuse readers—or even change your meaning altogether. Here is a statement that most women will disagree with:

> *Woman without her man has no reason for living.*

The writer actually meant to say something else altogether, but neglected the punctuation:

Woman: without her, man has no reason for living.

A common mistake in business writing is to use quotation marks for emphasis: *This bolt will give you "superior" tensile strength.* The head of a large company once put quotation marks around a word in an important paper, and when his administrative assistant asked him why he did that, he replied that it was to stress the truth of the point. The assistant asked whether it would stress the truth if he were to register at a hotel as John Durgin and "wife."

17. Understate rather than overstate

Never exaggerate, unless you do so overtly to achieve an effect, and not to deceive. It is more persuasive to understate than to overstate. A single obvious exaggeration in an otherwise carefully written argument can arouse suspicion of your entire case.

It can be hard to resist the tendency to stretch the facts to support a strongly felt position. Or to serve up half-truths as camouflage for bad news. Or to take refuge in euphemisms. Whenever tempted, remind yourself that intelligent readers develop a nose for all such deceptive writing and are seldom taken in by it.

For the same reason, you should always round out numbers conservatively. Don't call 6.7 "nearly seven"—call it "over six and a half."

An obituary writer held an envelope to be opened only when H. L. Mencken died. The message, from Mencken himself: "Don't overdo it."

18. Write so that you cannot be misunderstood

It is not enough to write sentences and paragraphs that your reader can understand. Careful writers are ever alert to the possibility of being *mis*understood.

A student paper began:

My mother has been heavily involved with every member of the California State Legislature.

While the writer's energetic mother was undoubtedly a clean-living lobbyist, some readers might have misunderstood the nature of her civic involvement.

Ambiguity often results from a single sentence carrying too much cargo. Breaking up your sentences can work wonders. Here is a statement from a report by the Nuclear Regulatory Commission:

It would be prudent to consider expeditiously the provision of instrumentation that would provide an unambiguous indication of the level of fluid in the reactor vessel.

If you break that idea into two sentences, and follow other suggestions in this chapter, you might end up with something like this:

We should make up our minds quickly about getting better gauges. Good gauges would tell us exactly how much fluid is in the reactor vessel.

19. Be alert to the sensitivities of minority groups and women

Our policy is to be sensitive but not hypersensitive. Many minority groups have strong feelings about the terms used to refer to them. As we write, you can use either "African American" or "black," but "Native American" is preferred to "Indian."

If by the time you read this, preferences have changed, so what? Use whatever happens to be the current preference of the group in question—and take the trouble to find out what that is. Minorities suffer enough without your labeling them with terms they regard as offensive, regardless of what you may think of their reasons.

24

In the preface, we touched on the issue of gender-specific language—the use of "he," for example, as a collective pronoun referring to women as well as men. We believe that you should avoid this old device assiduously.

"Every novelist hopes he will win the Pulitzer Prize" insinuates too strongly to today's readers that the writer is thinking only of male novelists. Better to write, "All novelists hope that they will win a Pulitzer Prize."

Another alternative is the time-honored "he or she"—as in "Every novelist hopes he or she will win . . ." That's okay once in a while, but becomes tedious with repetition. We avoid it as much as possible by converting the singular noun to a plural (as above). Or by other means—like changing from the third to second person: Instead of "when a reader picks up a memo addressed to him or her," you can write "when you pick up a memo addressed to you . . ."

In this book we have occasionally used "she" or "her" when we intend the reader to understand either a woman or a man, and in other cases, in similar constructions, we use "he" or "him." We believe that this scattershot method is clear to readers of both sexes and offends neither.

20. Use plain English even on technical subjects

Or perhaps we should say *especially* on technical subjects. The more technical the material, the less likely your reader will understand it unless you put it into the language we all speak.

An exception is when both writer and reader practice the same technical specialty. An advertising campaign for New York Telephone points up the difference. In one of the advertisements, a company's telecommunications director talks technical language to other telecommunications specialists:

> *Given the strategic significance of our telecommunication infrastructure, our fault tolerance to local loop failure left a lot to be desired.*

Here's how the ad says the company's chief executive, talking to the rest of us, puts the same point:

> *If the network goes down, the company goes belly up.*

What *Business Week* calls "technobabble" has aggravated just about everybody one way or another. "Plain English," says the magazine in a cover story, "is a language unknown in most of the manuals that are supposed to help us use electronic products." An example:

> *After pre-tuning, if you wish to change the real channel number to correspond to the actual pre-tuned station, press the CH No. SET button, after calling up the corresponding channel position number on the display and enter the desired channel number using the READ OUT buttons ("10" and "1") . . .*

And that's barely half the instruction.

If you're writing to lay readers on a technical subject, for heaven's sake test an early draft on a few of them. Finding out what's clear and what isn't can be valuable to you in editing. It can make the difference between success and failure in getting across what you want your reader to know, to understand, or to do.

Most murky technical writing is inadvertent, a sincere if doomed effort to communicate. Far worse is the deliberate effort to say something that you know readers won't like in a way that you hope they won't understand. We call this the techno-euphemism.

- *A nurse who dropped a baby referred in her report to "the non-facile manipulation of a newborn."*
- *The uncomfortable writer of an Air Force news release, reporting on a test of a Midgetman missile, said that "approximately 70 seconds into the launch an anomaly occurred causing the range safety office to initiate the command destruct sequence." Hiding in there is the news that something went wrong with the missile and they had to blow it up.*

Bad news is not made better by being baffling as well as unwelcome. When you spit it out in plain English, readers still may not like it. But their displeasure won't be compounded by the suspicion that you're trying to slip one past them.

When God wanted to stop the people from building the Tower of Babel, he did not smite them down with a thunderbolt. He said:

> *. . . let us go down, and there confound their language, that they may not understand one another's speech.*

He could think of no surer way to foil the project than to garble communications.

3

Writing on a PC or Word Processor

❧

Technical Note

For brevity we will refer to all machines that run word processing programs as "word processors." But the differences among such machines are worth considering if you are thinking of buying one primarily for your writing.

*The **word processing typewriter** is simple and inexpensive, a self-contained unit with a built-in program and a built-in printer.*

*The **PC (personal computer)** is more complicated to learn and costs a lot more. The PC also does more. It has a larger screen that shows many more lines of type, making it easier for writers. It can run any of several word processing programs, each with its own advantages and features. It can run other programs such as spread-sheets or data bases. It is faster in both input (what you type) and output (what you print), and it's compatible with many other computers.*

*A **laptop** is a compact PC that's worth its extra cost if you travel a lot and write while you're away. But it's harder for beginners than a desktop PC.*

We have yet to meet anyone who wanted to go back to a typewriter or writing in longhand after learning how to use a computer or word processor.

The word processor, with its somewhat familiar keyboard, may seem to be nothing more than a step in the evolution of the typewriter. It's a lot more than that. It's a whole other animal—a beast of burden that takes on the physical drudgery of writing, freeing us to put all our strength into the brainwork.

In his excellent book *On Writing Well,* William Zinsser calls the word processor "God's gift, or technology's gift, to good writing." But marvelous as these devices are, it's worth keeping in mind that they are machines and not magicians. They will not miraculously change a bad writer into a good one. They can even entrench a couple of the worst practices of bad writers.

In the rest of this chapter we will run through the ways you can enlist your word processor in your efforts to write well. And we'll put up a few warning signs to help you avoid the potholes and blind corners that word processors can strew in front of you.

How a word processor helps you improve your writing

David Halberstam, the author and journalist, puts it this way: "The word processor makes rewriting *fun.*" No longer is it a laborious business to change a word, add a point, delete a sentence, move a paragraph. Everything we declaim in this book turns out to be easy, even fun, to put into practice. Every woman and man a cursor virtuoso.

The advantages of a word processor are psychological as well as mechanical. When you know how easy it's going to be to make repairs and improvements later on, you can let your thoughts flow freely without interrupting yourself to fix things up as you go along. It's more like flying than writing.

On a word processor, the steps we urge in the chapter on editing become tolerable routine rather than grim duty. There can now be no excuse for failing to edit anything that comes off your desk.

How to take full advantage of your word processor

There are as many ways to write on a word processor as there are habits of writing. One writer likes to go back and correct after every paragraph or two, another roars through an entire draft without pause. No two people will find exactly the same set of practices suitable for their individual turns of mind. Your own proclivities will steer you toward what's best for you.

Longtime users, however, are in broad agreement on the merits of a number of procedures. Among them:

1. Write first, format later

Formatting is not writing. Playing with the details of the appearance of your paper can distract you from grappling with its content.

On the other hand, if you don't want your draft to be a shapeless jumble, it's a good idea to work from an outline—and to do just enough formatting at the outset to make your structure visible.

The drafter of this chapter, for instance, formatted the subheadings and the numbered points—all from the outline—as he typed the first rough version. This helped keep his thoughts in order as he went along. But going counter to his own advice, he also fiddled with indents and put the numbers and subheadings into boldface. They looked nice on the screen but wasted time and interrupted his train of thought.

If your word processor has a small screen with only a few lines visible at a time, it's a good idea to keep your outline in view on a piece of paper. It will help you to keep in mind how those few lines on the screen fit into your plan. If you have a big screen and a program with windows, put your outline in one of them and keep it in front of you.

2. Be paranoid about saving your file

If your word processor doesn't automatically and frequently save what you've written, you should do it yourself at least every fifteen minutes. Power surges, input errors, and other obliterators of your work are far from theoretical hazards.

3. To print or not to print?

How often you make a hard copy of your rough draft depends on the length and importance of what you're writing—and on your own working methods. The more important the paper, the more likely you'll want to compare drafts or refer back to earlier ones. While some programs make that possible directly on your computer screen, comparisons are often easier to read and to consider on side-by-side hard copies.

It's important to date or number your drafts. Some programs date every page automatically. If yours doesn't, you may find it easier and faster to do by hand, after printing.

4. Number your pages

With many of the less expensive word processors, the page numbers that automatically appear on your screen do not show up on your hard copies. Unless you go to the trouble of paginating every draft—often a nuisance—your drafts will come out of the printer with the pages unnumbered. This makes any document of more than a couple of pages maddeningly difficult to refer to in discussions with other people.

Never ever circulate any draft more than two pages long without numbered pages. There's nothing wrong with numbering them longhand if you find that easier, saving the printed numbers for the final draft.

5. Give thought to your file names

As your disk fills up, it becomes hard to remember the cute title you gave that letter. And a complicated hunt through everything on your disk will have you longing for the good old days of riffling through a file drawer.

You should develop a logical and easy-to-remember system for your file names. Professional writers think of their electronic file as a giant drawer with a small number of major directories, each divided into various subdirectories, and on to sub-subdirectories, and so on.

The current edition of this book was written on a word processor. WTW was the initial directory; CHAP01, CHAP02, the subdirectories for each chapter. In choosing your file names, prefer logic and simplicity to ingenuity. While the limitations on the number of characters you can use forces you to abbreviate, try not to do it to the point of obscurity. Your file should be a handy tool, not a puzzle or an amusement.

6. Proofread and then proofread again

"The word processor is an angel but it can't grant absolution," says free-lance writer David Swift. Because edited work looks so perfect on the screen, it's easy to be deluded into thinking that it really is. Here are some of the traps that snare even the most careful writers:

- Words left out.

- Accidentally repeated words or phrases. For some reason "and and" turns up a lot.

- Misuses that escape spell check. If you write "their" instead of "there," spell check won't know the difference. Same with "who's" and "whose" and dozens of other commonly confused words.

- Wrong tenses of verbs, nonagreement of pronouns.

- Punctuation mistakes—particularly forgetting to close quotes or parentheses.

It's a good idea to do your proofreading on a hard copy rather than on your computer screen. We're not sure why, but when you face a piece of paper like the one your reader is going to see, you become more alert to errors.

Caution

Your word processor may be clever enough to catch spelling mistakes and typos, but it is totally tolerant of more serious faults. It will even encourage some of them. Perhaps the worst is the tendency to overwrite.

In a column in *The New York Times,* Russell Baker bemoans the length of various kinds of writings these days and blames it on "the spread of the word processor which makes it so easy to write that people keep doing it long after their minds have bedded down for the night. This paragraph, written on a word processor and prohibitively long by newspaper standards, illustrates how easy the new technology makes it to keep writing long after the author has forgotten what he started to say, as I have at this point."

In the cartoon strip *Shoe,* a character sitting in front of his word processor replies as follows to an onlooker who has asked what he's writing:

Nothing so far. But the computer makes writing a lot easier, I'll say that. With just a flick of the finger I can write reams of nothing. I call it streams of unconsciousness.

Resisting streams of unconsciousness may call for a conscious effort. Good writers heed their outlines and stick to the point.

Since even a rough first draft can be made to look neat and finished on your screen, you can fool yourself into mistaking it for a polished masterpiece. The illusion may be magnified by the satisfying whirrings and clickings of your printer as it seemingly certifies that what you've written is all set for publication. In writing as in life, one is always wise to try not to be fooled by appearances.

Here are a few other cautions:
- *Be conservative in your choice of typefaces.*
  The most familiar faces are the most readable. For anything longer than a paragraph or two, roman (nonitalic) faces are more

readable than italics, and serif faces (like this text) are more readable than sans serif—like this.

This isn't a matter of taste or opinion. It has been proved over and over in studies of readership around the world.

Whatever typeface you choose, stick with it. You will not hurt the feelings of your program if you don't use all its faces in every paper. And you will save your readers' eyes.

There are many good standard typefaces available on most of the popular programs and printers.

* *Keep your fingers off the boldface and underline keys.*
  Boldface and <u>underlining</u> are fine for headings but should be used only for **occasional** emphasis in text. The same goes for *italics*.

  When you emphasize *too many* words, the effect is **not** what you intend. It may even be the *opposite*—when **everything** is emphasized, *nothing* is emphasized. And your page looks <u>messy.</u>

* *Forget about justifying type on the right margin.*
  Justified type on the right looks good in books and magazines because the spacing between words is handled with a lot of care. Word processors tend to do the job crudely, leaving artificially large spaces or else jamming the words too close together.

  Readers are accustomed to business papers with ragged right-hand margins. They look more natural, and are easier to read, than papers that have forced the margins into line. The narrower the measure, the worse the results.

Much as we believe in everything we've set down in this chapter, we don't want to push you into becoming a self-defeating perfectionist. "Perfectionism is spelled p-a-r-a-l-y-s-i-s," said Churchill. In some hands the word processor proves his point. Some people never stop editing. They never stop formatting. There is always one more change to try.

So our final word of caution is don't be too cautious—let 'er rip! The word processor is your liberator. Don't become its slave.

4

Business Memos and Letters That Get Things Done

❧

There are fewer memos these days and more presentation decks, fewer letters and more phone calls
(and electronic mail). Yet the written word is perhaps
more important in business than ever before.

Unlike a phone call, a memo or a letter can be
referred to over and over. You can study it, ponder it,
or pass it on to other people. Unlike presentation
decks, with their abbreviated bulleted points, memos
and letters are precise and require no spoken expla-
nation to fill in the gaps. They provide a record that
can refresh memories days or years later.

As the writer, you can express your ideas precisely, with every nuance just so. As the reader, you
can consider what's been written, when and where
you choose and for as long a time as you need.

Because of these assets, memos and letters are

versatile and valuable business tools that, when handled skillfully, can help you get things done.

How to write a memorandum

Memos are letters to people within your organization, or to people outside it with whom you work closely.

You are writing to *colleagues;* write in a conversational style. But an informal tone of voice is no excuse for sloppy thinking or careless expression. A confusing or ambiguous memo slows things down or messes them up.

Here are some suggestions on format that apply to all memos, and on how to handle certain kinds of memos that call for special care:

1. Put a title on every memo

Your title should never be tricky or obscure. It should identify—swiftly, and for all readers—what your memo is about.

A memo proposing an overdue raise for Tony Andrino should not be titled LONG OVERDUE—title it RAISE FOR TONY ANDRINO.

If you are responding to somebody else's memo, say so in your title:

FRANK OWEN'S JUNE 22 MEMO ON HOG PRICES

SEX-BLIND ADMISSIONS:
YOUR NOVEL IDEAS (MAY 3)

Don't worry about the length of your title—say as much as necessary to identify your subject:

POLLUTED RIVERS—MAJOR DIFFERENCE
BETWEEN COLORADO AND WYOMING

Center your title in capital letters over your message. It's easier for someone to spot there, thumbing through files or briefcase, than tucked off to the left along with the list of addressees.

2. List addressees alphabetically

If you list the people getting your memo in order of importance, you often run into complications. Is the head of manufacturing more important than the head of research? Who comes first among four assistant deans?

Such problems evaporate if you put *all* names in alphabetical order, except when that would be ludicrous. It would be ludicrous, for example, in a memo to the personnel director with copies to eight secretaries and the president, to list the president alphabetically among the secretaries. Put the president's name first; list the secretaries alphabetically.

3. Address memos only to the person who must take action

Send copies to the people you merely want to keep informed.

From: William Durwin   *copies:* Cindy Lee
   To: MARGARET BAKER   Sam Nasikawa
                               Bob Nieman

This says that Mr. Durwin wants Ms. Baker to *do* something, and the others just to know what's going on. If *several* people must do something, address the memo to all of them and make clear what each must do.

We prefer the full word "copies" to "cc," an anachronistic abbreviation for "carbon copies." And as an aside, we deplore the use of "blind" copies—copies sent behind the back of the addressee. As one business leader puts it, "You can tell how political a person is by the number of blind copies he or she sends out."

4. Make your structure obvious

Before you start to write, decide on structure. It will depend on the length, complexity, and nature of your subject.

Any memo longer than half a page requires a structure—*and the structure should be apparent to your reader.* Otherwise your memo will seem to ramble. Your reader will have a hard time remembering your points and how they hang together.

If what you want to say falls into conventional outline form—for instance, three main points, each supported by several examples, with a comment or two on each example—your outline will serve as your structure.

A clear structure helps your reader to remember your points. It also makes your memo easy to refer to.

Some memos are actually complex reports or recommendations, running a half-dozen pages or more. In any such memo, start by outlining what you're going to cover.

> *This memo is divided into three sections:*
> - *The problem*
> - *Four possible solutions*
> - *My recommendation*

Or write a brief covering memo and attach your report or plan as a separate document. This works well for major papers.

One useful structure is often overlooked: *a simple series of numbered points.* It has many advantages:

1. It suits your purpose exactly when you wish to make a number of loosely related observations on a single subject.

2. It eliminates the need to write connectives. When you're finished with one point, you plunge directly into the next.

3. It organizes your thoughts visually for your reader.

4. Your numbered sections can be as long or short as you wish. Some can be a single sentence, others two or more paragraphs.

   All that matters is that each number should indicate the start of a new and distinct thought.

5. The numbers make your memo easy to refer to.

5. End with a call to action

Say what you expect to happen as a result of your memo. Exactly what must now be done, by whom, and by when. Be specific.

If your memo raises questions, ask for answers by a specific date.

If your memo replies to questions raised by somebody else, simply stop when you're finished. Don't waste your reader's time with such homilies as "I hope this answers your questions." Since it goes without saying that you hope you've answered them, go without saying it.

If your memo is a report, draw conclusions from what you saw or heard or found out. Specify how certain you feel about your conclusions. Some will be beyond question, others purely speculative. Tell your reader which are which.

6. Send handwritten notes

Brief memos written by hand save time and by their nature are more personal and direct. Praise and appreciation can be especially effective in handwriting:

George:
That's sensational news about Acme. Get some rest now — you deserve it!

Susan:
Your report is superb. I'll react to your recommendations as soon as I get back from Fargo.

Since handwriting is personal, make sure whatever you write *sounds* personal.

7. Be careful with humor—or anger

Don't try to be funny in memos unless you are positive that all your readers will get the joke. That includes people who may not be on your list but might see a copy of your memo.

Avoid irony or sarcasm. Somebody will take it straight and get upset. People can brood for days over an innocently intended witticism.

As for anger, when you get angry in person, you leave nothing behind other than the memory of your behavior. When you put it in writing, you leave a *permanent record.* You may be sorry about that—after you cool down.

Angry memos do have their place. A good rule is to *write* it when you're angry, but don't *send* it until the next day, when you have cooled off enough to reflect on the consequences.

8. Should it be a memo at all?

An Italian proverb says: "Think much, speak little, write less."

The world is suffocating in paper. Often the kindest thing you can do for your reader is to give him nothing more to read at all.

According to one national survey, senior executives think that a third of their companies' written communications could be replaced by phone calls. As voice mail systems spread, the phone call becomes a practical alternative for jobs that used to be handled only by memos, like notifying a large group of a change in plans.

Sometimes the most efficient delivery of a message is still face-to-face, when you drop by somebody's office.

How to Write a Business Letter

1. Spell all names right

A misspelled name gets you off on the wrong foot. It suggests to the reader that you don't care, that you're a sloppy person. Check all names, no matter how much trouble it takes—on the envelope and in the letter. The names of individuals and of firms and organizations.

Use Mr. or Ms.—many people appreciate a touch of formality and nobody resents it. But leave it out

I have crossed out on the attached paper many unsuitable names. Operations in which large numbers of men may lose their lives ought not to be described by code-words which imply a boastful and overconfident sentiment, such as "Triumphant," or, conversely, which are calculated to invest the plan with an air of despondency, such as "Woebetide," "Massacre," "Jumble," "Trouble," "Fidget," "Flimsy," "Pathetic," and "Jaundice." They ought not to be names of a frivolous character, such as "Bunnyhug," "Billingsgate," "Aperitif," and "Ballyhoo." They should not be ordinary words often used in other connections, such as "Flood," "Smooth," "Sudden," "Supreme," "Full-force," and "Fullspeed." Names of living people -- Ministers or Commanders -- should be avoided; e.g., "Bracken."

2. After all, the world is wide, and intelligent thought will readily supply an unlimited number of well-sounding names which do not suggest the character of the operation or disparage it in any way and do not enable some widow or mother to say that her son was killed in an operation called "Bunnyhug" or "Ballyhoo."

3. Proper names are good in this field. The heroes of antiquity, figures from Greek and Roman mythology, the constellations and stars, famous racehorses, names of British and American war heroes, could be used, provided they fall within the rules above. There are no doubt many other themes that could be suggested.

4. Care should be taken in all this process. An efficient and a successful administration manifests itself equally in small as in great matters.

Churchill's memos got into the subject fast.

rather than get it wrong when you aren't sure what sex you're writing to and can't find out. Mickey, Terry, Gerry, Sandy, and many other names come on both girls and boys.

2. Get the address right

Check every detail. Mail addressed incorrectly seems slipshod at best, and at worst doesn't arrive.

Always put a return address on the envelope. The stamp might fall off, or God knows what.

3. Think carefully about the salutation

"Dear" is a convention we're stuck with. Odd and antiquated though it may sound, efforts to avoid it seem artificial, self-conscious, and downright rude.

What comes after "Dear" is worth some thought.

Use first names only when you're already on a first-name basis. Don't become anybody's pen pal by unilateral action.

Use titles—Dr., Judge, Professor, Senator.

An excellent but little-used alternative is to include both first and last names: "Dear Joan Larson." It is less formal than "Dear Ms. Larson," but doesn't presume personal acquaintance—like "Dear Joan."

This is an attractive way to address somebody you have met but who may not remember you. Or somebody important and senior to you whom you know only slightly. Or the other way around: Oscar Hammerstein II, the great songwriter, wrote "Dear Joel Raphaelson" in a letter to Raphaelson, then in college, about a review of *South Pacific* in the college newspaper, and it seemed entirely appropriate, both courteous and cordial.

4. Consider beginning with a title

Many business letters are parts of a long-term correspondence between seller and customer, attorney
and client, private firm and government bureau. In
such cases, it's a good idea to follow the salutation
with a title.

> Dear George:
>> Acme legal action: second phase

A title identifies the subject at a glance and is a
blessing for anybody who ever has to dig out previous correspondence on it.

Consider using a title even on one-time-only letters to strangers. No other opening so quickly identifies the subject of your letter:

> Dear American Express:
>> Lost credit card—Account #3729-051721

5. Make your first sentence work hard

Since titles on letters aren't standard practice, they
may strike you as too abrupt or too impersonal for
many situations. Then your first sentence has to per-
form the function of a title. Your reader wants to
know at once what the letter is about.

There is no need for the written equivalent of
small talk. The most courteous thing you can do is
spare your reader the trouble of puzzling out what
you're getting at.

Small talk

Dear Classmate,

As you know, we had a wonderful 15th reunion last
June. We can all be proud of the class gift we presented
at that time. Now we are well into the first year of the
end-of-the-century campaign.

Straight to the point

Dear Classmate,

It's time to pull together our 16th annual gift to the university. You'll remember we gave a whopper at our 15th reunion—but the need goes on.

What about letters responding to inquiries, or on a subject introduced in previous correspondence? Can you presume that the reader will know what your letter is about, having brought up the subject himself in an earlier letter?

Yes—up to a point. Here are two answers to a request for information:

Too windy

Dear Mr. Allen:

I am writing in response to your letter of June 24, in which you express an interest in the literature describing our line of herbicides, with particular reference to the control of dandelions in residential lawns. Unfortunately, we are all out of our pamphlets on this subject, but perhaps the following information will be of assistance.

Too abrupt

Dear Mr. Allen:

I'm sorry that we're out of the literature you asked for. Here's some information that may include what you need.

The letter on the right presumes too much. If Mr. Allen, who may write dozens of letters a day, doesn't happen to remember exactly what he wrote about to this particular firm, days or weeks ago, the first two sentences don't help him. He needs a speedy reminder of his inquiry—more direct than the first letter, less abrupt than the second.

Dear Mr. Allen:

We've run out of our literature on controlling dandelions. I'm sorry, and I'll send it as soon as a fresh
supply gets here. Meanwhile, maybe this information
will help.

The short first sentence reminds Mr. Allen of the
subject and tells him the chief thing he needs to
know.

Always identify your subject in your first sentence.

6. Stop when you're through

Just as some letters take their time to wind up and get
going, many slow down tediously before stopping.
Avoid platitudes like these:

Please call if you have any questions.

I hope this answers your concern.

Please give this matter your careful consideration.

Unless you have something to say that is more than a
formality, simply *stop*. If your last sentence says what
your reader would assume or do anyway, as in the
examples above, leave it out.

Such stuff doesn't sound sincere or friendly. It
sounds like what it is: routine formality. Your ending
won't seem abrupt if your tone throughout the letter
has been warm and personal.

If you want to add a personal touch, make sure
that what you say *is* personal, and something you
mean.

I've been reading about your heat wave and wonder
how you're getting along.

George, customers like you make this business worthwhile.

48

7. Be specific about next steps

If you want your letter to lead to action, your last paragraph should make clear what you would like that action to be. Or, if you're taking the action yourself, what you're going to do:

Vague	Specific
We're hoping to hear from you soon.	Please let us know your decision by August 1 so that we can meet your deadline.
I'm looking forward to getting together with you to talk more.	Are you free for lunch on Friday, July 17? I'll call that morning to confirm.

8. Use an appropriate sign-off

Gene Shalit, the television personality, signs all his letters "Thine." It's a personal trademark, like his bushy hairstyle. In general, though, your sign-off isn't the place to assert individuality. Keep it conventional and appropriate to your tone.

"Yours truly" benefits from a lack of any specific silly meaning. It is as rooted in convention as "Dear George," and useful for that reason.

"Sincerely" and "Sincerely yours" are all right if you don't mind proclaiming something your reader should take for granted.

So many people have latched on to "Cordially" that we have become numb to its mindless assertion of hearty friendship. Just don't use it on non-cordial letters: "We've turned your case over to our attorneys. Cordially. . ."

"Regards," "Best wishes," "All the best" are more personal than the others and less formal, but not appropriate if you don't know your reader.

And there isn't anything wrong with simply sign-
ing your name after your last sentence.

How to handle some common kinds of letters

Letters that ask for something

Say what you want, right away. Don't start by explaining *why* you want it. Your reader won't be interested
in your reasons before you reveal what you're asking
for.

Dear Mr. Sullivan:

Our problem | We are a new electronics firm and we
need to set up a department to do some
basic research.

Our thinking | Accordingly it occurred to our president,
Mr. Gene Schultz, that it would be a good
idea if we found out how some giant
Still hasn't | research departments such as the Bell
said what we | Laboratories were organized in the early
want | days.

Don't *start* by expressing your appreciation.

Dear Mr. Sullivan:

I would greatly appreciate your help on a
matter in which the Bell Laboratories may
be uniquely well informed.

Write that letter like this:

Dear Mr. Sullivan:

Says what we | Do you have any literature that spells out
want, and that | how the Bell Laboratories were organized
we'll pay | in the early days? If so, would you send it
to me and bill me?

Explains why	We're a small new electronics firm and your early experience might help us figure out the best way to set up our research program.
Thanks!	Your help would be invaluable to us.

That's the correct order for letters of inquiry: *first,* what you want; *second,* who you are and why you want it; *third,* an expression of appreciation for favors to come.

If you're asking for routine information—a copy of a published speech, records on your bank account, a price list—you can leave out the reason you want it and shorten your thanks.

How to say no

No, we don't have a job for you. No, we won't give you more credit. No, we don't agree that it was our fault and that we owe you a refund. No, we can't get your order to you in time for Christmas. No, we won't publish your story. No, we can't contribute to your charity.

Turning somebody down in writing may seem easier than doing it in person, but in some ways it's a lot harder. It is less personal and more permanent.

Readers can't see the expression on your face. Nor can they hear the tone of your voice. Nor can they ask questions on the spot about things that puzzle them or that they take issue with.

Your letter has to compensate for those disadvantages:

- It must be as *clear* as you would be in person.

- It must be as *tactful* and *understanding* as you would be in person. Pay close attention to your tone.

- You must anticipate your reader's questions and objections and do your best to answer them.

Put everything in your letter to this test: Would you say it and would you say it in that way, if you were face-to-face with your reader?

"We regret to inform you that . . ." is the standard opening of millions of "no" letters. It is hard to imagine anybody ever *saying* "I regret to inform you that . . ." You'd say "I know how disappointed you're going to be, but there just isn't any way I can do that" or "No, I don't think that will be possible—but how about this as an alternative?"

Let's say you're the manager of a store that sells refrigerators. After using your top-of-the-line model for almost three years, a customer has reported that it conked out on a hot weekend when he was away, and that he returned to find all his food spoiled.

He wants you to replace the refrigerator with a new one, free, and to charge nothing for the service call that put his back into commission—only temporarily, he fears.

Here is how some people would respond:

Dear Mr. Traggert:

An institutional thumbs down

I regret to inform you that we are unable to accommodate your request for a new refrigerator. Our repairman reports that the trouble was minor and is unlikely to recur.

What a dope you were!

At the time of purchase, you were offered a three-year service contract. Had you accepted it, our service call would have cost you nothing additional.

Our hands are tied | But since you did not accept it, we are required to charge you for the service.

Boy, do we sound sincere | I sincerely regret any inconvenience this episode may have caused you and hope that you will now get many years of satisfactory service out of your Model 6034-Y.

Yours truly,

A turndown like this, with its chill, corporate tone, is all but guaranteed to lose a customer for your store.

If you were to hear Mr. Traggert's story at a dinner party, you wouldn't say "That episode may have been inconvenient for you." You would respond spontaneously with something like "That's *awful*—what a way to come home from a weekend!" Why not start your letter in the same human way?

Dear Mr. Traggert:

How terrible for you to come home from a weekend and find all the food in your refrigerator spoiled. I can imagine how you must have felt.

The reader now knows that at least you appreciate his predicament. You might continue in the same vein:

Agreeing is better than arguing | I quite agree that any refrigerator—and particularly a deluxe model such as yours—should give you trouble-free service for a lot longer than three years.

Puts problem in perspective | However, no manufacturer's system of quality control is perfect—which is why we advise our customers to invest in a service contract.

53

Appeals to reader's sense of fairness. Note use of first person	If I were to charge you nothing for your service call, you would, in effect, be getting the benefits of a service contract without having paid for it.
Seriously considers reader's request. Gives full reasons for turning it down	In considering your request for us to replace your refrigerator, I have talked to the repairman who fixed it. He assures me that there is nothing fundamentally wrong—the problem was caused by a freak failure of a common bolt, which he has never seen happen before. He feels it is most unlikely to recur: "A million to one against it," he said.
Even the turndown is sympathetic	I don't think a new refrigerator would be any more likely to give you the years of service you have every right to expect.
Leaves door open	But should you have further trouble, I hope you will get in touch with me at once.

Yours truly,

In this letter, the author shows a personal interest in the customer's situation. He treats the demands as reasonable, and takes the trouble to explain why he is turning them down. He leaves channels of communication open—-just in case. In short, his letter sounds as though he cares.

Never say no in anger—no matter how angry the other party may be. *You* are in the position of power. Control yourself. Always appreciate the feelings of the person you are turning down.

Never belittle anybody—never make a request or a complaint sound foolish or unreasonable. Always show consideration for points of view other than your own.

Never say no casually, in an offhand manner. Always take the trouble to explain your reasons.

All of this applies just as forcefully to a *form* letter. Do everything you can to make it sound as little like a form letter as possible.

The admissions officers at Princeton have to turn down nearly nine thousand applicants every year. The writer of this form letter was sensitive to how his young readers would feel about the bad news:

Dear Ms.____:

The admission staff has completed its selection of the Princeton Class of 198—, and I am afraid that I must report that we shall not be able to offer you a place.

Since each candidate presented a unique set of credentials, this letter cannot possibly explain the reasons for each decision. Let me assure you, however, that our decisions were not reached quickly or easily and that, because of the highly competitive nature of our admission process, we had to disappoint many applicants who were qualified to do the work at Princeton.

Needless to say, in making our decisions we do not claim to possess either special wisdom or infallible judgment. Because our task has been to select from nearly 11,000 applicants those 2,150 who we think will best comprise a class that is both excellent and diverse, we have had to turn down thousands of talented and interesting people. We have tried to be as fair as possible with all applicants, and our decisions should not be interpreted as judgments passed upon either their innate worth or their ability to contribute to society.

I hope it will not seem out of place if I add here a personal observation about college admissions. The importance of this spring is not that you have been admitted to some universities and colleges and denied admission to others, but rather that you are ending a major portion of your life and beginning another. The years ahead will be filled with academic and personal challenges that can be both frightening and exhilarating, and with those years there will come a new sense of independence and maturity. In the final analysis, it is not primarily the institution you attend but rather your desire to learn from and with other people that will make college an exciting and fulfilling experience.

With best wishes,

Sincerely,

A clear and considerate letter written with sympathy for the feelings of the reader. That's the secret of how to say no.

How to collect money owed you

It's hard to write a good collection letter. You don't want to irritate your reader. But you do want to get the money.

Watch your tone of voice

If you're reminding somebody that a payment is a few days overdue, don't sound as though you're about to call in the lawyers.

Bad	Better
Dear Mr. Jones:	Dear Mr. Jones:
It has come to our attention that you have failed to remit your June payment, which became overdue on June 12.	I'm writing to let you know that your June payment (due on June 12) hasn't reached us yet.

On the other hand, if you *are* going to take legal action, don't pussyfoot around. Come right out and say what you mean:

Dear Mr. Hinson:

Your June payment is now three months overdue. You have not responded to three letters in which I asked if you thought there was an error in the bill. I cannot reach you by telephone.

Therefore I'm asking our lawyers to collect the $104.56 that you owe us.

Watch your choice of words

Never use words which suggest that your reader is a criminal. "Delinquent" is a favorite of righteous bill collectors, as in "You have been delinquent in meeting your payments for two months in a row."

Your object is to collect; irritating your readers is not likely to send them to their checkbooks.

Don't imply that your reader is a *liar.* If a woman has written you that she paid her bill promptly on the first of each of the last four months, and you have received no payments, don't write "You claim that you paid your bill each month . . ."

The word "claim" reeks of disbelief. If she *is* lying, it won't help. If she *isn't,* it will infuriate her.

Better to take her at her word and suggest a positive next step:

Dear Ms. Bossler:

Assumes truthfulness | Although you've been mailing your payments promptly, we have no record of receiving them.

Admits possibility of own error | Perhaps the error is in our records. Since you have been paying by check, your bank will by now have returned two and perhaps three of your canceled checks, if in fact we have deposited them.

Suggests constructive action	Please look for them and if you find them, send us photocopies at our expense so we can set our records right.
Asks for payment courteously but firmly	If you *cannot* find the canceled checks, we must assume the payments somehow got lost. Would you then send us a new check covering at least the first three payments, and preferably all four?
Reduces likelihood of yet another "lost" check	I enclose an addressed, stamped envelope. Yours truly,

There is nothing in such a letter to irritate an innocent customer; nor is there any loophole for further delay on the part of a guilty one. Keep in mind that your purpose is not to make your reader angry, but to get the money that's owed you.

How to complain

Never write just to let off steam. Write to get something done—your money back, or faster service, or a mistake rectified.

Is the person who will read your letter at fault for what went wrong? If not, there's no point in getting sore in your letter. While anger has its place in correspondence as in life, more often than not you'll get better results from a cool, lucid statement of what's gone wrong and what you'd like done about it.

Include *everything* your reader needs to know to take action—account number, item number, pertinent dates, form numbers, photocopies of canceled checks, photocopies of bills.

If you leave anything out, you may have to wait through another round of correspondence before you make progress.

Put your complaint and what is wanted in the first sentence.

The sweater I ordered for my son's birthday never arrived. Please send another immediately.

Ask for a reply with a specific statement of what the next step will be:

Please let me know what action you plan to take, and when.

If you are not the person who handles this, please get my letter to the right person at once. And please let me know that you've done so, and who it is. I'd appreciate that information by Friday, May 10, at the latest.

Be clear. Be complete—and you can toss in a heart-rending description of what you have suffered. Be firm. Be courteous. That's the kind of letter that usually gets the fastest results.

If it fails, raise hell. Write to the head of the organization and include all correspondence. Nine times out of ten you'll get satisfaction from the boss.

How to answer complaints

Never be defensive. If the complaint is reasonable, say so—and say what you're going to do about it.

Neiman-Marcus, the Dallas-based chain of department stores, has built much of its reputation on its responsiveness to customers. Here is how Chairman Richard Marcus replied to one customer's complaint:

Dear Ms. Klugman:

Accepts the complaint at face value

I am astonished to learn of the shoddy service you recently received from our Mail Order Department, and there is no excuse for the lack of response and discourteous conversation you had with a member of our Mail Order phone staff.

Says what he's going to do about it

I'm asking Mr. Ron Foppen, senior vice-president and director of our Mail Order operation, to investigate this matter immediately, and he will personally contact you within a few days.

Apologizes

I apologize for any inconvenience and embarrassment we may have caused you,

Asks for continued business

and trust that we will have the opportunity of serving you better in the future.

Yours sincerely,
Richard Marcus

Far from being defensive, Mr. Marcus comes right out and calls the store's service "shoddy" and says that "there is no excuse" for it.

The entire letter is personal, sympathetic, and responsive.

What if you feel that the complaint lacks any justification? Say so, but be courteous.

Intelligent readers are good at detecting the slightest hint of irritability or impatience. You should be at least as courteous on paper as you would be in person. Forthright and direct. Never sarcastic or rude.

When to use very short letters

A short letter—sometimes no longer than a sentence or two—can be highly effective.

It can establish your interest.

Dear Mr. Woodrow:

Your proposal interests us a lot. We'll get back to you as soon as we've sorted out our budget problems for next year—no later than the end of next week.

It can let your reader know what's happening, and demonstrate your thoroughness.

Dear Ms. Pruitt:

Half your shipment went out this morning, air express. The other half follows next Monday, parcel post, as you requested.

It can say thank you.

Dear Helen:

I hope you can keep Dan Murphy on our account forever. He's the best sales representative I've ever dealt with.

Note on electronic mail and faxes

More and more written communications go back and forth electronically, through computer systems. This speeds things up. And, at least in theory, it eliminates the problem of lost or misdirected mail—although a memo lost because you hit the wrong keys, or because the power blipped, is a lot more lost than one that's parked temporarily in the wrong slot in the mailroom.

Whether on a computer screen or on a piece of paper, good writing is good writing and bad writing is bad. The same principles apply. If sending your message electronically encourages you—as some claim it does—to write in a more informal person-to-person style, so much the better.

There is one disadvantage to electronic mail, and it can be serious. Unless the recipient of your message goes to the trouble of printing it out—and often that means on a printer half a block away—there is the likelihood that it will be read through once and, with a stroke of the "file" or "delete" key, will disappear from both screen and consciousness.

We suggest that if you want action as a result of an electronic message, you should take extra trouble to be both specific and emphatic about what you want done and by whom and by when:

ACTION THIS DAY

Lorna and Bill:

I must have your opinions on this proposal by 5 tonight at the very latest. If for any reason that's impossible, please let me know by return mail, the minute you have read this.

Some experienced hands advocate *starting* electronic memos with a declaration of what you want done. This tends to snap the reader's attention into focus.

Perhaps the greatest boon of electronic mail is that it gets rid of those stacks of paper on your desk. But that's also its shortcoming. Your reader has nothing to stick in a briefcase or to make a note on, or to refer to quickly when you call to discuss what you've written. All this makes it more important than ever for the writer to be clear, to get to the point fast, and to place as small a burden as possible on the overloaded memory of the reader.

You might also want to bear in mind that few electronic mail systems are as *secure* as they purport to be. Apart from flaws in the system, a slip of the finger can broadcast your private memo to the entire staff. If you want to make sure it's private, put it on a piece of paper and stick it in an envelope. (And deliver it by your own hand!)

Faxes

There is a lot to be said for sending messages by fax, and very little to be said against it. Compared to a phone call covering the same ground, a fax will nearly always cost less because it will take less time— no need to inquire about the heat wave out there on the coast. And it provides both you and the recipient with a full and accurate record of your message.

A fax is cheaper and faster than overnight courier service. It's incomparably faster, and generally more reliable, than ordinary mail—and except for long documents, not a great deal more expensive.

The main drawback is the public location of most office fax machines. Unless you know that you're transmitting to somebody's private machine, you should not send anything by fax that you wouldn't want broadcast.

There is no special technique for writing faxes— the fax is the medium, not the message. But you do need to pay attention to how you number and label your pages. If you send a four-page paper with a one-page covering note, the fax machine will number the covering note Page 1, the first page of your paper Page 2, the second page of your paper Page 3, and so on. This can get confusing when you start referring to the paper in meetings or conference calls.

The best way to avoid such confusion is also the best way to make sure that pages of your message don't get mixed up with other faxes pouring out of the receiving machine. Label and number every page prominently and in detail, top center:

PAGE 3 OF 4-PAGE PROPOSAL TO OPEN DENVER OFFICE FROM EXPANSION COMMITTEE TO J. L. BRADY

It seems laborious, but it will preclude gnashing of teeth at the other end of the line.

When typing something for a fax, leave plenty of space in all margins—top and bottom as well as left and right. Half the faxes we get arrive with words or lines chopped off.

5

Sales Letters and Fund-raising Letters

❧

The remarkable growth of direct mail has been triggered by several mini-revolutions—the advent of sophisticated computer models and better mailing lists, the convenience of credit cards and 800 numbers, dual-income households and accompanying changes in life-styles and shopping habits.

While changes in technology have been a large part of this revolution, what hasn't changed is what to *say* to people to get them to respond and send money.

The two kinds of letters you are most likely to be asked to write are *sales letters* and *fund-raising letters,* subjects about which many books have been written. Here are some of the things professionals do to get people to part with their money, starting with some broad principles.

The first principle: it pays to test

Many organizations fly by the seat of their pants and don't know what is working and what isn't. The joy of direct marketing is its accountability. The reader responds directly to the writer or organization; you count the money that comes in and you know how you've done.

Which leads to the first principle: *Test*.

It is common to find that one mailing will produce many times the response of another for the same product. It pays to test if you plan to mail to a substantial number of people, or if you plan to mail more than once.

Testing is not just for large organizations. You can devise simple low-cost tests by coding responses and counting them. If you cannot test, take advantage of the testing of others. When you receive the same mailing over and over, year after year, you can be reasonably sure it has been proven in testing. Study it.

Don't assume anything. And prepare to be surprised.

- Many people will read long letters and on a wide range of subjects. Long letters often pull better than short ones.
- Some months (or even weeks or days) are more productive than others for some kinds of mailings.
- Sometimes a higher price will produce more response than a lower one.
- People will respond again and again to the same mailing. Don't change for the sake of change. Only change a successful mailing when testing has given you a proven winner to replace it.

Important—test only one change at a time. If you test several, you won't know which helped (or how much).

The second principle: estimate how much you will get

To decide how much to *invest* in each potential customer, you must know or estimate how much each customer is *worth*.

If you expect people to send money just once, the calculation is easy. Will you get back enough money to cover the cost of the mailing plus the cost of the merchandise—and leave you with a profit? If yes, go ahead. If no, start again.

Most direct mail is in a different category—it goes to people who may buy more than once:

- Customers whose repeat orders you can reasonably expect
- Subscribers—to magazines, books clubs, record clubs, art clubs—who are likely to renew their subscriptions or send in new orders
- Contributors to schools or hospitals or any local charity or cause, who might well give again in future years

For this kind of customer, you can invest heavily in your initial mailing—even if it loses money the first time around, as it often does.

What works best in sales letters— tips from the professionals

1. Get to the point quickly

Much direct mail is read over a wastebasket. Guess what this letter is about—and what's likely to happen.

Dear Friend:

I receive, as no doubt do you, a fair number of letters asking for attention and not least for money. All, as I've often said, tell me at undue length what I already know or do not need to know. The wonderful computer errors of the Republican National Committee apart, I try to read and respond as appropriate. Nonetheless, I yearn for brevity. Not doubting that you share this yearning, I will be brief.

Compare it to the opening of this letter, which ran for years and beat all alternatives:

Quite frankly, the American Express Card is not for everyone. And not everyone who applies for Cardmembership is approved.

Start fast.

2. Make sure the offer is right

The professional direct mail writer works on the coupon first—not the letter. What is the offer? How should it be stated? What are the terms?

The offer is what gets the action.

It may be a reduced price, a premium, a charter subscription, a ten-day free-trial offer, or a combination of these.

The National Audubon Society offered a membership package of outings, bird walks, workshops, films, lectures, discounts on books and stamps and prints, and a subscription to Audubon Magazine. All for annual dues of $18.

Small changes in an offer, or even in the way the offer is presented, can make an immense difference in response. If you test nothing else, test your offer.

3. Get people to open the envelope

Always say something on your envelope; it is what your prospects see first. Tease them. Hint at your offer. Tell them about a gift inside—or about valuable information.

ADVANCE NOTICE

PLEASE OPEN AT ONCE:
DATED MATERIALS INSIDE

WE HAVE A FREE GIFT FOR YOU

RECEIVE FOUR ISSUES FREE

4. Have a strategy

A sales letter is an advertisement delivered in the mail. Successful advertising starts with clear thinking on what to say—and to whom.

Try to form a picture of your prospect—in terms of age and income, life-style and attitudes, the products he or she uses. Then determine the single most important benefit your product or service offers. Most have several benefits, but one must be more important to your prospects than the others. The essence of a successful strategy is sacrifice; you must play down lesser benefits to concentrate on the one with the most sales power.

5. Favor long letters over short ones

Most amateurs assume people won't read more than a page or two at most.

The fact is that long letters pull better than short ones—if:

- you have an attractive offer
- you grab the reader's attention at the beginning
- the letter is loaded with relevant facts

Look at the mailings you receive. How many are just one page, and how many are several pages long—and include several pieces of literature?

One of the largest and most successful direct marketing companies, Publishers Clearing House, sends a package that includes six enclosures plus a letter almost 1,000 words long. You are asking your readers to make an investment—in time, money, or both—and must convince them that what you're selling is worth it.

6. Give something away

You'll be amazed how something free, however small, can add to the power of a sales letter. You can offer a free first copy, special discounts, a free membership certificate, a free pin, free trials.

A simple pamphlet, perhaps one you've already printed for another purpose, can be an effective free offer—and a cheap one.

7. Make it inviting to read

People won't read long letters that look formidable, with long blocks of text.

> *Use visual devices—to make your letter look inviting and interesting, and easy to get through: inset paragraphs (like this), crossheads (like "Make it inviting to read" above), handwritten notes in the margin.*

Think beyond standard envelopes and standard sizes of paper. The most effective mail is often an unusual size, shape, or color.

8. Make it look like the real thing

Letters should look like letters, not like advertisements. Coupons should look like coupons (or money), certificates like college diplomas or high-grade bonds.

Coupons and certificates are conventions that

readers understand at a glance. Making them look like something else, to be different, defeats their purpose.

9. Don't let the reader off the hook

People procrastinate. You must create a reason for your prospect to act *now.*

> *The allocation of Collectors Edition Sets makes it necessary to accept reservations on a "first come, first served" basis ... and under no circumstances can reservations be accepted if postmarked after August 30.*

> *Why not send the application and deposit now? We expect the courses to be filled fast, so don't delay.*

Danny Newman, America's most successful seller of subscriptions to concert and theatrical seasons, builds all his mailings to a single injunction: SUBSCRIBE NOW.

10. Add a postscript

The P.S. is one of the best-read parts of any letter. Use it to remind the reader of some important detail, to restate your offer, to create a sense of urgency with a deadline or a special premium.

> *P.S. I've touched on this before, but I know tennis players, so let me emphasize it: You'll get all the tennis you can sop up. Even during the evening (if you're up to it)—the courts are available for free play.*

> *P.S. I've also been asked to tell you because of the limited printing of the premiere issue, we may not be able to send additional first issues, or accept Charter Subscriptions, after April 15.*

Why not try a P.S.? It doesn't cost any more.

"The more things change..."

Who's Mailing What?, a newsletter published in Stamford, Connecticut, conducted a study of 66 mailing packages that have beaten all alternatives for a minimum of three years, some for more than a decade. The similarities are striking.

The overwhelming majority used techniques and elements that have been around since the 1930s.

- The basic elements include a letter, a brochure, a reply card, and a short second letter highlighting the offer of the gift.
- Forty-three of the 66 mailers offer something for nothing, or a discount.
- Letters addressed to the busy executive (whom we are often told has no time to read) averaged three pages.
- Sixty of the 66 offered a bill-me option.

If the advances of technology are astonishing, so too is the consistency of these great mailings—proven by testing.

What works best in fund-raising letters

In the world of political fund-raising by mail, two acknowledged masters are Richard Viguerie, a conservative, and Roger Craver, a liberal. Craver disagrees with Viguerie on every issue, observes *The New York Times,* "except on how to write a letter."

> *"You need a letter filled with ideas and passion," says Craver. "It does not beat around the bush, it is not academic, it is objective. The toughest thing is to get the envelope open. The next toughest thing is to get the person to read the letter."*

A Craver letter for handgun control carries this message on the envelope:

ENCLOSED: Your first chance to tell the National Rifle Association to go to hell!

The letter starts:
Dear Potential Handgun Victim

To raise money for charitable, educational, or political causes, you must appeal to the emotions. People can have strong feelings about the causes represented by a community fund, about a political candidate, about a religious institution. They want to give. Yet those new to fund-raising are often hesitant about asking for money.

The first truth to remember when raising funds is this:

Most people don't give because nobody asked.

Which leads to this corollary:

Never ask anybody for money until you yourself have given.

When you have given—and given until you have caused a change in your personal budget—you feel more comfortable about asking others. Your appeal rings true.

Epsilon Data Management, an expert in direct mail fund-raising, makes the stakes clear:

Your organization's survival depends on how well you identify, acquire, and retain donors.

The value of a donor stretches over many years. The renewing donor will provide financial support to your organization year after year.

Epsilon goes on to quote a study that indicated that over 80 percent of total private giving in the United States was attributable to the individual donor. So direct mail is a crucial source of funds for charitable institutions.

Here are some principles:

1. Cultivate previous donors

People who have given previously are the best source of funds. Epsilon's experience is that 60 percent of first-year donors will renew in Year Two, and 80 percent of retained donors from Year Two will renew *each subsequent year.*

Often those donors will increase their gifts. They may participate in deferred giving programs. They will even help acquire new donors by working as volunteers.

These facts are at the heart of direct mail fund-raising; they lead to two central conclusions:

- *It pays to dig in your pocket to get new donors.*
  A donor who gives once is likely to give again.

  New Yorkers who give to the Red Cross typically give seven times in ten years—and increase their gift 20 percent during this period. Thus, the true value of a donor is not the initial $7 average gift, but closer to $60. With this knowledge, the Red Cross was able to afford giving a free first aid manual to first-time givers—even though the mailing didn't pay for itself with the first donation.

- *It pays to invest in building a relationship.*
  Donors are believers, and believers give. You can go to them on a regular schedule or in emergencies.

  Write to them regularly, and keep them informed about the organization and its activities. Make them members, not just givers. Send membership certificates and pins. Then, when it comes time to renew their support, they need only an inexpensive reminder to prompt their generosity and loyalty.

Write to say thanks. Thanks, *and won't you give again?*

2. Make it personal

People don't give to faceless institutions; they give to other people. Put your appeal in personal terms.

Use your letter to report interesting information—like shop talk among colleagues—as well as to ask for money. Describe the work your institution is doing, and tell readers why it is important. Use case histories.

Tell readers the bad things that are going to happen—unless they give. Don't let them assume the drive will be successful whether or not they give. This adds urgency to your appeal.

> *Unless we hear from you right away, we may be forced to close down two Morgan Memorial buildings.*

3. Tell the prospect how much money you want

The reader does not know how much money you expect. Suggesting the size of the contribution is up to you.

One useful method is to tell readers what different services cost, so they can select a giving level. The Lyric Opera of Chicago gives this approach a stylish twist with a letter to Santa Claus from the general director.

> *Santa, it would be lovely if you could leave an $8 million check in my stocking this year—but I know that's a bit*

much to ask. So let me list some of the things we really do need, that maybe you can help us with.

Children's Back Stage Tour ($7,500)

Senior Citizen's Matinee ($15,000)

Orchestra scores and vocal parts ($2,500 per opera)

Air fare to bring artists from New York ($325 each)

Ballet shoes ($75 each)

Wigs and make-up for the chorus of Mefistofele *($5,500)*

Leaves to redecorate the tree in Elixer of Love *($550)*

Rental of keyboard for sound effects ($3,607)

Youth Education programs ($15,000)

If I listed everything Lyric needs, or needs money to fund, this letter would go on for pages—so I've selected only a few items that are especially on my mind as the holidays approach.

Don't forget to tell people how little you spend on administration.

Finally, assure them that you mean it when you say no contribution is too small, even a dollar. Giant oaks from little acorns grow.

Build trust

Nobody likes a mailbox full of junk mail. However, one person's junk is another's passion. Some people cannot get enough garden catalogs or cookbooks or whatever. Junk mail is mail which is inappropriate— because it is talking to the wrong person, talking at the wrong time, or using the wrong tone.

People read direct mail and they act on it—if the product or service or cause is something they want or believe in, and if they trust the mailer. The single most important thing you can do to raise money through the mail is to convince people that they can trust you.

Never exaggerate, either in word or picture, what you are offering, or when you will deliver, or any other detail. If, for some unforeseen reason, you can't live up to a promise, send a postcard saying so; apologize; and say what you're going to do about it. The trust you build will be well worth the extra cost.

6

How to Organize Plans and Reports

❧

The best report ever written may have been Julius Caesar's *Veni, vidi, vici.*

> *I came, I saw, I conquered.*

Some reports, like Caesar's, describe the outcome of an operation. Most say *what's happened so far and where things stand.*

A plan states *what to do.*

The consequences of faulty organization and careless writing are severe. Reports land in wastebaskets, unread. Plans go straight to the files, unacted on.

How to write a plan

"For Montgomery," wrote a biographer of the British field marshal, "it was all a question of having a plan.

Once you had decided what you wanted—what, in military terms, was your aim—you made a plan, which you then implemented carefully by stages, maintaining the aim and concentrating all your resources to achieving it."

Whether you are writing a battle plan or a long-term strategic plan or an annual business plan or a reorganization plan, your objective is the same: *action*.

1. State your goal

A plan should start with a clear statement of purpose:

> *The Central Park Conservancy wants heightened visibility—to gain credit for what it has accomplished in order to raise more money to maintain what the Conservancy has restored (and to restore more of Central Park).*
>
> *The assignment, then, is to determine strategy and plans for communications and marketing.*

Now that your audience has your goal clearly in mind, everything in your plan should pertain to it. Cut out all irrelevancies. If you feel you have to touch on secondary or side issues, label them as such.

The readers to keep in mind are those who will have to decide whether to approve your plan, send it back for more work, or reject it. Anything that confuses them or throws them off the track makes approval less likely.

2. Summarize all pertinent facts

The sort of facts to include will depend on the nature of your plan. One plan will dwell on the historical setting, listing past successes and failures. Another will lay out sales revenues, performance against budget. A third will focus on economic or political conditions. Many plans will call for a combination of such data—and lots more besides. Cover everything that bears on a decision.

Any fact that's relevant should have a place on your summary.

3. Draw principles from your facts

You can almost always infer one or more principles from the facts—lessons learned, either from the situation at hand or from others with analogous facts.

Show how your facts bear on the action you're proposing. Never parade facts on their own, single file. Don't leave your reader with an argument that, like a Mexican pyramid, doesn't come to a point.

4. State the steps you propose to take— and your reasons

A plan is a recommendation until it is approved. Then it becomes a commitment to action. It describes, step by step, exactly what is supposed to be done. The Central Park Conservancy plan presented recommendations—and ideas for implementing them—in five categories:

- *Strengthening communications basics*—employee motivation programs, a graphic look and theme, a Central Park Bulletin.

- *Becoming more intimate with the neighbors*—corporations within a five-minute walk, nearby hotels and retail businesses.

- *Opportunities for revenue*—Summer Stage, Paul Simon concert, private parties, permits for film and TV shoots, a walking tour audiotape, products for children (coloring books, birthday parties, tie-ins with F. A. O.

Schwarz), leveraging the park as a tourist destination.

- *Marketing programs*—a marketing committee, an integrated advertising and direct mail campaign, membership programs.
- *Turn up the PR volume*—inviting morning news shows to broadcast live, a film for movie theaters, encouraging local TV weathermen to broadcast live from the park, an annual radio telethon tribute to John Lennon.

5. Anticipate objections

Any good plan considers alternatives and risks. It anticipates questions and answers them.

Don't cover up problems. Face them squarely. This makes your proposal realistic—and makes *you* realistic. "I never promised you a rose garden."

6. Never settle for a first draft

The first draft of a major plank in U.S. policy after World War II came through in a weakly worded, bureaucratic style. Several drafts later, it emerged as a ringing credo that became known as the Truman Doctrine.

First Draft for Truman Speech

It is essential to our security that we assist free peoples to work out their own destiny in their own way and our help must be primarily in the form of that economic and financial aid which is essential to economic stability and orderly political processes.

Final Speech

I believe that it must be the policy of the United States to give support to free peoples who are attempting to resist subjugation by armed minorities and forces.

I believe that it is essential to our security that we assist free peoples to work out their own destiny in their own way.

I believe that our help must be in the form of economic and financial aid.

How to write a report

Reports cover events large and small—meetings, trips, analyses of competition, developments, good news, bad news.

Some reports aid the planning process; some come after it, reporting on progress or results. Good ones obey the following principles:

1. Involve your reader

Why are you writing the report, and *why should anybody care?* Remember the reader, laden with bulging briefcase.

Good reports get the reader's interest in the first sentence:

This reports on a management meeting at which a new salary policy was decided.

The purpose of this report is to assess new competition—a product that could cut our sales in half.

2. Include first-hand observations

Before you draft your report, get out in the field and see for yourself what's going on. A field trip often gives you more realistic answers than any amount of statistics. Or it can lead you to the right questions to ask back in the office.

Generals often go to the front—a personal visit gives them a feeling for what's going on, against which to judge the thousands of facts that pour in.

Field trips are often a source of ideas. Just as

important, they add the breath of life to your reports. An intelligent appraisal of actual conditions can be essential to progress. Report what is happening out there, and what you think should be done about it.

3. Separate opinion from fact

A little boy in a newspaper cartoon says to his father, "I asked you for the facts of life, but what you're giving me is opinions."

Both facts and opinions are important; make clear to your reader which is which.

Facts are facts, regardless of who is reporting them: "It's 24 degrees and the wind is from the northwest at 15 miles an hour." Opinions vary depending on the observer: "It's a pleasant winter day—brisk and bracing."

You should never leave your reader in doubt as to which is opinion and which is fact.

Opinion stated as fact	Opinion stated as opinion
The information would be useful, but would cost too much to obtain.	We'd all like to lay our hands on that information, but none of us thinks it's worth what it would cost.
We can't get started by May 1.	To get started by May 1 I suspect we'll have to go heavily into overtime.

The way you deploy your facts can give weight to your opinion. Include the principal facts necessary to support your views. Face up to those that weigh against you. But don't throw in unnecessary or irrelevant details just to show you've done your homework.

Facts are facts. Conclusions and recommendations are always *opinion*.

How you *choose* facts, and how you marshal them,

may well reflect the point of view that you're advocating. But your report will stand up better, especially should it come under fire, if you make a conscious effort not to lump your facts and your opinions into a single undifferentiated pile.

4. State the facts fully and accurately

Newspaper reporters are trained to do this with the famous five Ws—who, what, when, where, why (or how). Not a bad discipline for a writer of reports—who is, literally, a reporter.

> *The major findings are that Homebrand sales are off 28 percent, distribution is down 20 percent, and Alien's new product is being purchased by nearly half of all heavy users.*

All the facts, unpleasant as well as pleasant.

Never inflate the validity of your facts. If you only visited ten stores in two cities, don't refer to an "extensive store survey."

5. Interpret the facts

What conclusions do you draw from the facts? What principles can you relate them to? What action do they suggest?

Some reports are purely for the record. Others—the most important ones—are designed to lead to action.

6. Give your report a structure

Whether you start with a recommendation which you then support with facts, or lay out the facts before making your recommendation, your reader should know *where you are going*.

Here is a structure that often works:

Purpose—why the reader should pay attention.
Summary—no surprise endings.
Findings—what facts can you marshal?
Conclusions—what patterns do you see?
Recommendations—what action do you propose?

Each section should be labeled clearly.

7. Make it short

There is no need to parade *all* your information unless the reader needs every detail to understand your report.

Put only those facts that are essential to your point into the body of your report. Relegate charts and supporting data to an appendix.

8. Keep your purpose in mind

Every report is written for a purpose. A report titled "Alternative Paths to Persuasion" tells readers:

This report looks at studies from the social sciences that reveal some conditions under which people's preferences and behavior are influenced without their conscious awareness. We focus on these studies not because we believe all decisions are always or even partly non-rational, but because they sometimes *are. As we are in the business of persuasion, we should understand what goes on.*

With the purpose of the report clearly set forth, the writer took care that everything that followed was relevant.

There are many kinds of reports with many kinds of purposes.

A *conference report,* for example, has only one purpose: to record decisions taken at meetings. It does not restate arguments or report praise or blame.

It records what was shown or discussed. What

was decided (not why). What action is required and who will be responsible for it. When it is due. What money was authorized. It covers actions and decisions—nothing else.

A *competitive report* covers competitive activity, a *progress report* covers progress, and so on.

9. Always take notes

Never trust your memory when collecting material for a report. Write down everything you want to remember.

> *"The horror of that moment,"* the King went on, *"I shall never, never forget!"*
>
> *"You will, though,"* the Queen said, *"if you don't make a memorandum of it."*
>
> Alice's Adventures in Wonderland

The best reports are written by people who take the best notes.

10. Make it readable

The annual reports of U.S. corporations typify what most people think of as impenetrable business writing—turgid, bureaucratic, impersonal. And most people accept that such a style is in the nature of these reports, and that nothing can be done to make them more readable.

Most people—but not Warren Buffett, Chairman of Berkshire Hathaway, whose reports are admired for their literate insights as well as for the financial results they disclose. A typical Buffett report explained his reason for favoring long-term investments over frequent shifts from one investment to another.

We have found splendid business relationships to be so rare and so enjoyable that we want to retain all we develop. This decision is particularly easy for us because we feel that these relationships will produce good—though perhaps not optimal—financial results.

Considering that, we think it makes little sense for us to give up time with people we know to be interesting and admirable for time with others we do not know and who are likely to have human qualities far closer to average.

That would be akin to marrying for money—a mistake under most circumstances, insanity if one is already rich.

Berkshire Hathaway also takes the trouble to make the *numbers* readable, proving in passing that there is no conflict between intelligibility and success.

Our gain in net worth during 1989 was $1.515 billion, or 44.4%. Over the last 25 years (that is, since present management took over) our per-share book value has grown from $19.46 to $4,296.01, or at a rate of 23.8% compounded annually.

Buffett was appointed interim chairman of Salomon, Inc., after dubious practices got this eminent Wall Street firm into some scaldingly hot water. A couple of months later, double-page newspaper ads carried Salomon's third-quarter results and a report to shareholders from the interim chairman. We will quote a number of excerpts from this report, which exemplifies the kind of business writing that we encourage throughout these pages.

A few Salomon employees behaved egregiously—a fact that will prove costly to you as shareholders—but the misconduct and misjudgments were limited to those few. In short, I believe that we had an extremely serious problem, but not a pervasive one.

During my tenure as Chairman, I will consider myself the firm's chief compliance officer and I have asked all 9,000 of Salomon's employees to assist me in that effort. I have also urged them to be guided by a test that goes beyond rules: Contemplating any business act, an employee should ask himself whether he would be willing to see it immediately described by an informed and critical reporter on the front page of his local paper, there to be read by his spouse, children, and friends. At Salomon we simply want no part of any activities that pass legal tests but that we, as citizens, would find offensive.

Our pay-for-performance philosophy will undoubtedly cause some managers to leave. But very importantly, this same philosophy may induce the top performers to stay, since these people may identify themselves as .350 hitters about to be paid appropriately instead of seeing their just rewards partially assigned to lesser performers . . . Were an abnormal number of people to leave the firm, the results would not necessarily be bad. Other men and women who share our thinking and values would then be given added responsibilities and opportunities. In the end we must have people to match our principles, not the reverse.

I believe that we can earn . . . superior returns playing aggressively in the center of the court, without resorting to close-to-the-line acrobatics. Good profits simply are not inconsistent with good behavior.

We admire what Buffett says—and how he says it. So, apparently, does corporate America; by the end of the day the ad ran, four of the eleven big corporations which had suspended dealings with Salomon had returned to the firm.

7

Add Force to Presentations and Speeches

&

$\mathbf{R}$ight or wrong, more and more business is conducted in meetings. One thing that's *never* right is an incompetent, mumbling presentation or speech that wastes time, bores the audience, and fails to persuade.

Presentations and speeches that are forceful and persuasive have two things in common—they are sensitive to the audience, and they start with a point of view.

People have a terrible time knowing where to begin in writing a presentation or speech. The answer is not to hunt for a great opening. Nor to ask around for the latest joke. *It is to decide what you want to say.*

How to write a presentation

The presentation—with its omnipresent "deck" or flip charts—is a writing form of its own.

You are writing for an audience in a conference room, not for individual readers. A presentation is a visual show. Mastering it can be as important to your career as any other form of business writing.

1. Know your audience

Don't fly blind. Try to get briefed on everybody you'll be talking to. Anticipate what they will be thinking.

Each audience is different and has special interests. Take them into account. If you use a presentation many times, don't repeat it without *some* change.

2. Start with specific, written objectives

Everything you say, everything you show, every device you use must move you toward your objectives. Almost everyone has been to big show-biz presentations at which the entertainment overwhelms the message.

Keep things simple. Keep them on target.

3. Open with a headline stating your theme

You need a theme to give your presentation unity and direction, and to fix your purpose in your audience's mind. Make it a simple theme, easy to remember, and open with it.

DOUBLE YOUR SALES

CUT YOUR COSTS

NEEDED: A NEW BALL PARK

MORE FUN FOR BOSTONIANS

Tie every element in your presentation to the theme. If you're using charts, put the theme all by itself on one chart and place it where it will be visible throughout the presentation.

4. Show an agenda

Tell your audience what you are going to cover, all your major points.

Describe the structure of your presentation, and say how long it will take. Estimate time conservatively—err on the long side rather than the short side.

A presentation that is promised for 20 minutes and goes 25 seems like an eternity. The same thing promised for 30 minutes seems short in 25, crisp and businesslike.

Throughout the meeting, refer to the agenda—and your theme—to keep your audience on track.

5. Talk about your audience, not about yourself

While you are talking about *your* credentials and *your* achievements, the people in the audience are thinking about *their* organization, *their* business, *their* problems. Try to use their organization's name more often than your own.

Relate what you offer to your audience's needs. Present everything possible in terms of benefits to the audience.

6. Use your imagination

Look for creative visual devices—interesting ways to present dry, routine materials.

> *Pie charts and bar charts are more interesting than columns of bare numbers. Symbols can be even better—for example, increasingly large pictures of a company's headquarters building to indicate growth of earnings. New computer software programs make charts easy.*

News magazines hire top artists to make their charts interesting and clear. Study their techniques—and borrow from them.

Think of ways to involve your audience. Play games with them. Invite your audience to guess the answers to questions, or to predict the results of research—before you reveal them.

7. Do everything that's been asked—
and a little more

Be precise in covering what was requested. If you cannot cover some point or other, say so and say why.

Try to add something extra, something *unexpected*. It demonstrates more than routine interest. Play tape recordings of customers describing your audience's product. Quote a relevant passage from a speech your audience's chief executive made years ago. Show an excerpt from yesterday's TV news that illuminates or reinforces an important point.

8. Use numbers and headings
to guide your audience

Number your main points on charts or slides, and tell people how many you have.

Head each new section to help your audience follow you.

STRATEGY

1. Small markets before large ones.

2. Three new markets every six months.

3. Concentrate construction in spring and summer.

---

9. Prepare for questions

As you're writing, be alert to your inevitable weak spots. What are the holes in your argument? What alternatives did you consider? What prejudices does your audience bring to the meeting?

If you cannot build the answers into your presentation, be ready to handle them—briefly and respectfully, so the questioner will feel smart to have asked.

10. Finish strong

Don't let a meeting drift off into trivia. Close with a summary and a strong restatement of your proposition or recommendation.

For major presentations, look for a memorable, dramatic close—something visual, perhaps a small gift that symbolizes your main point.

At the end of a presentation on the importance of hiring the best people, everybody around the meeting table was given a Russian doll—one of those wooden dolls that come apart in the middle to reveal a smaller doll inside, which in turn contains an even smaller doll, and so on. Inside the smallest doll, each person found a slip of paper with this message:

If you always hire people who are smaller than you are, we shall become a company of dwarfs.

If, on the other hand, you always hire people who are bigger than you are, we shall become a company of giants.

"Oh, give me something to remember you by" goes the song. As soon as you've gone, your audience is likely to turn its attention to other things—perhaps to presentations competitive to yours. Leave something to remember you by.

How to use visual aids

Slides or charts? If you have the choice, think it over carefully.

Big meetings almost always require big screens—and therefore slides. If you're more than 12 feet from your audience, it is hard to get charts big enough to be read by everybody in the room.

Slides are seductive. Dramatic photographs, big type, color—all relatively cheap. Charts are harder to handle. They are not so colorful or dramatic. They often cost more.

But beware! Slides require you to turn down the lights, focusing attention on the screen rather than on you, and giving the meeting a formal tone. Another danger is the darkness-induced temptation for the audience to drift into a brief nap.

People are interested in people. It often pays to keep the lights on and work with charts. The audience then stays alert and gets to know you.

New computerized multimedia capabilities open up whole new presentation opportunities—the visuals of slides (and films) combined with the lights-on virtue of charts.

The following principles apply equally to slide, chart, or multimedia presentations:

Read every word on the screen or chart to the audience. Don't paraphrase. Don't comment as you go along. Read it all.

Some presenters think it is unnecessary, even childish, to read verbatim. But no matter what *you* do, your audience will read what's in front of their eyes. If you are saying something else, you will distract and confuse them.

Once you've read everything up there, you can

comment on it or expand on it. You will no longer be competing with your slides or charts for your audience's attention.

If your style is to ad-lib, put only key words or phrases on your charts or slides.

PROBLEMS

1. Price

2. Quality control

3. Japan

4. Sweden

Face the audience. Your script should repeat everything that's on your slides. This allows you to work from it; you don't have to turn to the screen. If you want to indicate individual items on slides, use a pointer.

Prepare a presentation book the audience can keep. Tell them at the start that you'll give them copies of all slides and charts in a book after the meeting. This will relieve them from taking notes. You'll get their full attention.

Keep your promise about how much time you'll take. Running longer than you said you would at the outset shows a lack of discipline, and cuts short the time left over for a question-and-answer session that could tip the decision your way.

Presenters often sprout wings and fly when confronted with an audience. They expand, tell anecdotes—and hate to sit down. If what you've written is exactly on time in rehearsal, you'll probably run over in performance. If you're planning to take 20 minutes, write for 15.

Rehearse—always with props. You may think you know how you're going to handle your charts and other visual materials, but each presentation seems to present problems of its own. If you can, rehearse in the room where the presentation will take place. Plan everything—even the lighting.

Edit—to shorten. Reorganize—to make sure your message is clear. Revise—to make it sound like you, speaking naturally.

Go through your entire presentation at least twice. Only an amateur worries about overpreparing and losing an edge. The better you know what you're doing, the more spontaneous you'll seem.

How to write a speech

Author Tom Wolfe reports a dramatic example of freezing at the prospect of writing for an audience. *Esquire* magazine had asked him to write about the makers of custom cars in California—an early 1960s phenomenon—and he just couldn't get started.

When the deadline approached—and still not even a *beginning*—the managing editor, Byron Dobell, instructed Wolfe to type out his notes for another writer to turn into the story. Wolfe found himself typing those notes as a personal letter to Dobell. He put down "Dear Byron"—and then something happened.

Says Wolfe: "Words started pouring out, without my thinking of literary forms. I was writing for *one guy.*"

Dobell crossed off "Dear Byron," put the notes without change into *Esquire,* and Wolfe had found his voice as a writer.

Addressing "one guy" rather than a faceless audience is a helpful principle to keep in mind when you write a speech. What you write should sound exactly like you talking to *somebody.*

Think of your audience and your subject, decide what *single* point you want them to take away, then start writing. Put down anything that gets you into what you want to talk about, no matter how clumsy it seems. Don't worry about it yet. Get rolling; polish later.

It helps to immerse yourself in your subject long before you write. Read and think about it, and make notes—including actual lines that might be used in the final speech. Then put together a broad outline of three or four major points, each with three or four subpoints. Then go back to your notes and see where they fit in the outline.

One trick that often works: cross out the first several paragraphs. You'll find your opening line halfway down the first page. Most of us have a tendency to warm up too long before throwing the pitch.

Perhaps the most important rule is not to accept any topic that you don't feel strongly about. Tom Peters, author of *On Excellence,* considers it the one golden rule:

> Stick to topics you care deeply about, and don't keep your passion buttoned inside your vest. An audience's biggest turn-on is the speaker's obvious enthusiasm.

Some principles for writing speeches

1. No speech was ever too short

Most good talks take less than 20 minutes. Consider what you have so often had to sit through, and how much better it could have been said in fewer words. When Theodor Geisel, creator of the Dr. Seuss books, was awarded an honorary degree by Lake Forest College, outside Chicago, he was determined to respond with the best speech ever—and the shortest. "Kids hate long speeches," he said. "They have other things on their minds at graduation." Here is his entire talk:

My Uncle Terwilliger on the Art of Eating Popovers

My uncle ordered popovers
from the restaurant's bill of fare—
And, when they were served,
he regarded them
with a penetrating stare . . .
Then he spoke Great Words of Wisdom
as he sat there on that chair:
"To eat these things,"
said my uncle,
"you must exercise great care.
You may swallow down what's solid . . .
BUT
you must spit out the air!"

———————————

And
as you partake of the world's bill of fare,
that's darned good advice to follow.
Do a lot of spitting out of hot air.
And be careful what you swallow.

Few of us—indeed only one of us—have Ted Geisel's talent. But it doesn't take talent to figure out what you want to say, to say it, and to sit down.

2. Form a picture of the speaking situation

Is it an after-dinner address, a lecture, a seminar? Are you the only speaker or one of several? Whom do you follow on the program? Will the audience be sleepy?

Keep the situation in mind as you write. It will make a difference in what you say as well as in how you say it.

3. Start with a point of view

Think about *what you want to say*. The president of the National Education Association knew exactly what he wanted to say at the Advanced Criminal Law Seminar.

> *My topic is "Education or Incarceration?" That's neither a threat nor a promise. It's a fairly accurate, if somewhat simplistic, description of the choice before America's young people.*
>
> *For the fact is that young people who fail to graduate from school—or who graduate without the skills today's economy demands—almost certainly will end up in low-wage jobs or unemployed. They are likely to lead lives of poverty, desperation, and crime. They not infrequently end up in jail.*

H. L. Mencken compared two speeches by President Harding. The first was on the simple ideals of the Elks:

> *It was a topic close to his heart, and he had thought about it at length. . . . The result was an excellent speech—clear, logical, forceful, and with a touch of wild, romantic beauty. . . . But when, at a public meeting in Washington, he essayed to deliver an oration on the subject of Dante Alighieri, he quickly became so obscure and absurd that even the Diplomatic Corps began to snicker.*

Ideas that you believe in make good speeches. It helps to keep a speech file with fodder for your talks.

4. Avoid clichés

It may be "an honor and a privilege" to have been invited to speak, but that is not what people came to hear you say.

Plunge into what you want to say. That's what your audience wants to hear.

5. You don't have to tell jokes

Are you funny? In small groups, do you make people laugh? If not, forget it.

If you do tell a joke or anecdote, don't build up to it ("On the way here tonight . . ."). Tell the joke. Make sure your jokes are relevant to your point. Make sure they're *funny*—by trying them out ahead of time.

6. An interesting title promises an interesting speech

Your title should reflect your point of view—and should sound interesting. A tip-off to the lack of a point of view in a speech is a lazy title or no title at all. "Remarks Before the Seventh Annual Conference."

The title of a speech is different from the title of a movie or a book. It should be interesting but for a different reason. Movie titles are designed to sell tickets, book titles to sell books. You, however, will already have your audience, there to hear your speech as a professional duty. But the less it *feels* like a duty and the more it can be anticipated with plea-sure, the more likely you are to get full attention and to register what you want to say. An interesting title can create that sense of pleasurable anticipation.

Here are some good titles:

Leadership: The Forgotten Factor in Management
The Boob Tube Gets Smart
Keep Listening to That Wee, Small Voice
Somewhere West of New Jersey
World Class Quality: Different Cultures—Common
    Language

Nonprofits: Five Additions to the Ten Commandments
How to Keep Your Ads Out of Court
A Dollar Saved Is a Dollar Burned

7. Write your speech to be spoken

Don't think of it as an oration. Think of it as a conversation with a friend—even if you are addressing a joint session of Congress, as playwright Vaclav Havel did in his role as president of the newly freed Czechoslovak Socialist Republic.

The last time they arrested me, on October 27 of last year, I didn't know whether it was for two days or two years . . . I had no idea that two months later I would be speaking in front of this famous and powerful assembly, and that what I say would be heard by millions of people who have never heard of me and that hundreds of politicians and political scientists would study every word I say. . . .

But I have not come here to speak for myself or my feelings, or merely to talk about my own country. I have used this small example of something I know well, to illustrate something general and important. . . .

After outlining eight specific political implications of the velocity of change in Central and Eastern Europe and in the Soviet Union, President Havel then considered responsibilities of intellectuals like himself, in the same person-to-person way of speaking:

I've only been president for two months and I haven't attended any schools for presidents. My only school was life itself. Therefore I don't want to burden you any longer with my political thoughts, but will move on to an area that is more familiar to me, to what I would call the philosophical aspect of those changes that still concern everyone, although they are taking place in our corner of the world.

Before your final draft is typed, read it *aloud* several times—and edit it until it sounds like you talking naturally.

NOTE: Ghost writers can help, but your speech must ultimately reflect *you*. Never deliver a speech drafted by someone else before you have revised it to sound like you.

8. Leave them thinking

If you start with a single point you want your audience to take away, conclude with a memorable way for them to do so. Don't just repeat it ("As I said at the beginning of this talk . . .") but find a vivid image to register the point. Here's First Lady Barbara Bush at a Wellesley College commencement:

> *For over 50 years, it was said that the winner of Wellesley's annual hoop race would be the first to get married. Now they say the winner will be the first to become a C.E.O. Both of those stereotypes show too little tolerance for those who want to know where the mermaids stand. So I want to offer today a new legend: The winner of the hoop race will be the first to realize her dream . . . her own personal dream. Who knows? Somewhere out in this audience may even be someone who will one day follow in my footsteps, and preside over the White House as the president's spouse. I wish him well!*

A great speech is one that inspires the audience to think about a subject from a fresh perspective.

How to Deliver a Speech Effectively

Think about speeches that have impressed you. The speaker seemed to be *talking* to you, not *reading* to you. You've got to establish contact with the audience. And that means looking out at the people, not down at the script.

Some speakers have a bag of tricks that make it easier for them merely to glance at the speech now and then and spend most of their time looking around at the people in the room. Ultimately, however, the only way to do this is to *rehearse*. Rehearse what you have to say over and over until you know it almost by heart.

What sets the memorable speaker apart from the ordinary one is confidence and presence. As somebody's mother-in-law says, "You get right up there and pretend you're just as good as anyone else."

The better you know your speech, the more spontaneous you will sound. And the more confident.

It's difficult to be objective about your own speaking ability. But it can help to listen to yourself rehearse on a tape recorder. Better yet, take the traumatic step of seeing yourself on videotape. A convincing teacher.

The most effective speeches and presentations sound as if they have been spoken, ad-lib, and not written down at all. Great presenters and speakers make it all sound so easy and so natural that one assumes it just pours out of them. It almost never does.

It sure is encouraging to have such a terrific turnout for Direct Response Day. If the size of this audience is any indication, the direct response business is booming.

And some new figures we have suggest that it's going to keep on booming, as you're going to see in a little while. But first I thought I ought to tell you something about how we laid our hands on those figures, so you won't doubt their reliability when we go through them. It took us a lot of time and work. And it cost us a lot of money.

As a matter of fact, It cost my company $40,000 to send me here today -- and that doesn't even include my airplane "refreshments," as they're called. $40,000 is what we spent to find out what I should say. That's about $1,500 for every minute I'm up here, so I hope I have your attention.

We used the money to make some phone calls last November. We called up 1,541 people -- half of them women, half of them men, all of them adults. It was a nationally representative sample.

We asked them 113 questions about whether or not direct response advertising affects their lives -- and if it does, how it does.

Lopping off two paragraphs improved this speech.

8

Recommendations and Proposals That Sell Ideas

❧

You may well have to sell your ideas in writing. In written recommendations to your bosses to take some action. In written recommendations to committees or boards. In written proposals for the funding of grants.

Their purpose is to persuade somebody—or, more often, a number of people—to buy an idea: to approve it and agree to put it into action. But many proposals leave their audience confused about what is being proposed. Others are clear enough, but unpersuasive. Some even dissuade by casting doubt on the value of the project (or the competence of the proposer).

Some sell too hard. Henry Kissinger was quoted as saying of State Department memos that they give you three options: The first leads to nuclear war, the second to unconditional surrender, and the third is what they want you to choose.

Coming up with good ideas is only a first step. Unless you are able to sell your ideas, you might as well not have had them.

Recommendations

All organizations spend a large amount of their time preparing and then considering recommendations to do one thing or another. When preparing a recommendation, there are two pervasive problems to keep in mind.

The first problem is that you have been living with the subject and your audience has not, or at least not with the same intensity. You have to bring them up to speed before you can persuade them.

The second problem is that you are usually in competition with other recommendations for finite resources. Yours must be *more persuasive* to carry the day.

Here are some principles for making a persuasive case:

1. Think of it as selling—not as presenting

Just laying out your views is not enough. You must marshal both logic and passion behind your facts.

Anticipate your audience's reservations and face them squarely. Instill confidence that you have thought hard about potential pitfalls, and are fully prepared to guide the venture around them safely and successfully.

2. Tell people where you are going

Your first paragraph should quickly establish both your subject *and* its scope. The strategy for Harry

Truman's successful campaign for the presidency in 1948 was outlined in a 43-page memo. The first paragraph made clear its ambitious scope.

The aim of this memorandum is to outline a course of political conduct for the Administration extending from November, 1947, to November, 1948. The basic premise of this memorandum—that the Democratic Party is an unhappy alliance of Southern conservatives, Western progressives and Big City labor—is very trite, but it is also very true. And it is equally true that the success or failure of the Democratic leadership can be precisely measured by its ability to lead enough members of these three misfit groups to the polls on the first Tuesday after the first Monday of November, 1948.

3. Put your recommendation in context

Persuasive recommendations usually include a section on background. The purpose is to tell or remind the reader of prior meetings or information into which this recommendation fits.

To help the board of managers of the New York Botanical Garden understand the background for its recommendations on improving overall effectiveness, a management consulting firm summarized its activities with a detailed list:

Reviews with the staff of major programs and functions; analysis of financial records, interviews with Board members; visits to three other botanical gardens; comparison of the Board structure and fund-raising activities with those of other comparable New York institutions; preliminary interviews with foundations, corporations and government officials to gauge the outlook for future funding.

With this impressive background in mind, the audience was prepared to accept the report's findings, conclusions, and far-reaching recommendations.

4. Recommend—and do it early

This is a recommendation, not a story with a surprise ending. Busy people don't want to guess what you're leading up to, so get to the point quickly and clearly.

We propose that a new environmental program be launched within six months.

The committee recommends a new organizational structure to focus more on clients and markets.

Most recommendations involve a degree of pain—a new and expensive investment, or a difficult decision. Delaying the bad news is not going to help. Get it up front.

5. Lay out specific reasons in support

The rationale for your recommendation is the heart of your argument. What is the evidence?

To forestall a likely client worry that "nobody reads long copy in advertisements," Ogilvy & Mather cited numerous cases of long-copy ads that had produced terrific results:

- A single British Travel Authority advertisement attracted 25,000 responses. BritRail, a primary cooperator, reported "its best sales year ever in the U.S."
- A campaign for International Paper drew a thousand letters a day commenting on the advertising or requesting reprints.
- For Cunard, an advertisement with 26 separate items of information paid for itself four times over in direct sales.

Specifics persuade. They must be relevant and impressive—every one of them. A chain of specifics is no stronger than its weakest link; the weak one will attract the attention of your critics in the audience.

6. Anticipate questions—and consider reframing them

It's always wise to anticipate questions that are likely to be asked. But sometimes a probable question doesn't strike at the heart of the matter. In such cases, reframe the question.

In our example in the previous point, the anticipated question was "Does anybody read long copy?" The recommendation reframed it so that the reply would reveal what the questioner actually needed to know: "Does long copy really sell?"

7. Cover all the bases

A memo of recommendation should be complete in itself. The classic style (attributed to Procter & Gamble) includes these headings:

- *Purpose*
- *Background*
- *Recommendation*
- *Rationale*
- *Costs and timing*
- *Next steps*

It is even more persuasive if you can outline alternative recommendations and describe why they are less attractive.

8. Lead people through with headings

You know where you're going, but the audience doesn't know unless you tell them. It is helpful to give some clues along the way. A recommendation to advertise on television headed each section clearly:

WHY TELEVISION?—It's Media Smart

- *It Provides the Needed Extra Impact*
- *It Extends the Person-to-Person Print Campaign*

WHAT DID OUR RESEARCH SHOW?—Review of Objectives and Methodology

- *Television Findings—Breakthrough Quality was Key*
- *Television Shifted Respondents' Perceptions*
- *Television Proved Unique Advantages over Print*

WHAT IS OUR CREATIVE RECOMMENDATION?

- *TV Goals*

9. Emphasize the benefits of your recommendation

There must be a payoff in a reasonable time if your recommendation is to be accepted and acted on. A recommendation by a management consultant emphasized these goals:

- *To achieve sustainable competitive advantage in cost, technology, and systems quality.*
- *To reach an appropriate return on investment.*
- *To maintain the highest levels of customer satisfaction.*
- *To improve the use of key people.*

The recommendation went on to show how those objectives would be met.

Never fail to answer the main question your audience is asking, however silently: *"What's in it for me?"*

10. Give your recommendation a title

Not just a descriptive title but one with a benefit. A presentation on writing to a law firm was titled:

10 WAYS TO WRITE BETTER, SAVE TIME, AND
COMMUNICATE MORE EFFECTIVELY WITH CLIENTS

You don't have to tip your hand about the exact nature of your recommendation, but you should at least involve your reader in your subject.

11. Summarize

For long recommendations, it's helpful to start with an executive summary. Include all main points, a sentence or two for each. Let the full document fill in the details.

Proposals

Foundations and government agencies who grant money have a special problem: They have to say no far more often than they say yes. There are simply more applications than money. Your job is to deprive them of excuses to say no to *you*.

Federal agencies usually require you to fill out an array of application forms; proposals for foundations allow for more flexibility. With either, it is possible to stand out from the crowd. And there will be a crowd.

Put colorful detail in your proposal. A successful proposal by Dartmouth College's Hood Museum for a grant for a major exhibition, "The Age of the Marvelous," started with a narrative:

> *During the 16th and 17th centuries, European culture was marked by an intense fascination with the Marvelous, with those things or events that were unusual, unexpected, exotic, extra-ordinary or rare.*

It went on to outline, in colorful detail, the themes and content of the proposed exhibition:

> *What were the sources and historical antecedents for the Marvelous?*

> *Why did an interest develop in objects that aroused surprise and wonderment?*

What was considered a Marvel? What were the criteria by which something (especially a work of art) was judged to be Marvelous?

The waning of the Marvelous.

Make it urgent. The introduction of a proposal by the National Academy Foundation identified the urgent need for an educated work force to participate in the advancement of the U.S. economy in an increasingly global marketplace.

> *A review of recent educational findings reveals that we are far from developing such a workforce or even one on parity with that of other industrialized nations. For example, we find that American schoolchildren are typically found at the bottom of international comparisons of mathematics and science, and the majority of students seeking Ph.D. degrees in mathematics and engineering from American universities are from foreign countries.*

The thought that must be communicated is that the project might not happen if there is no funding. "You can make the difference," is one way to get a yes.

Do your homework. Most funding sources have published the criteria against which they make their decisions. Show how your project fits.

Include a letter. While federal agencies require a formal application, there's no rule that says you can't attach a strong statement in your own style, to bolster your proposal.

Identify the problem your project solves. The opening paragraph should frame both the issue and the benefit. Start fast.

Put the money in context. Outline the total program budget—and the amount being requested for this specific project. The National Academy Foundation proposal cited earlier puts a price tag on each of its projects:

- *Producing a Banking and Credit course for the Academy of Finance—$28,000.*
- *Pre-Academy curriculum for younger students—$30,000.*
- *Student scholarships—$10,000 each.*
- *Seed grants for Academies of Public Service—$15,000 to $20,000 per school.*

Credibility is important. How long have you been around? What is your track record? It's not enough just to establish the importance of your project. You must persuade your reader that you can make it happen.

Less is more. Be realistic in what you hope to accomplish. Better to identify a specific problem that you might actually solve than to give the feeling that you are trying to cure all the ills of society.

Identify a specific, measurable outcome. Define the problem clearly, then set objectives related to what you plan to accomplish. The proposal of a cancer research institute identified both the probable and possible benefits of its project.

> *The focus of this NIH Proposal is an improved understanding of the factors responsible for the growth of human germ cell cancer, a curable solid tumor . . . Using cellular, biochemical, immunologic, pathologic, and recombinant DNA techniques. . . .*
>
> *From these studies, a better knowledge of the role of growth factors in the growth or differentiation of germ cell cancers will be gained. Application of the findings may lead to improvements in the diagnosis and treatment of this solid tumor based on biologic and genetic properties.*

What happens after the money is spent? For continuing programs, it is important to present a plan that will assure some kind of continuing support after the grant runs out—so the program doesn't die.

It need not be dull. A successful proposal, by the South-North News Service, to fund a world affairs newspaper and teachers' guide for U.S. secondary schools, opened with an arresting image.

> *Oh, to be 14 years old!*
>
> *The rigid antagonisms of the Cold War are crumbling . . . The white power structure of southern Africa is coming face to face with reality . . .*
>
> *But survey after survey shows us that neither the 14-year-olds nor their teachers can find Vietnam or Brazil on a map, or tell the difference between Tel Aviv and Cairo, or label the Indian Ocean or Antarctica.*

The first requirement is to get read.

What it takes to persuade

Most decision-makers—the audiences for recommendations and presentations—have to say no most of the time. They don't like to say no, but they just can't say yes to everything. There is a limit to any organization's resources and money.

After years of looking at recommendations and proposals, we conclude that most of them are easy to turn down because their authors don't organize their material persuasively.

Typically there are a series of points, often numbered to give the appearance of structure. But the presenter does not relate the points to each other, does not fit them together to make a case. Points are not supported by evidence. Facts, while impressive in themselves, don't bear on the argument.

There is a relentless logic in every successful proposal and recommendation. Everything ties together strongly in a cohesive whole, like a well-told story. It starts by setting the scene, to establish a frame of reference for what is to follow. Then it brings in relevant and undisputed facts to lead people along and get them nodding in agreement. Finally, it prepares the audience to accept how the story ends—what you want done.

To persuade, every sentence must move your audience along irresistibly to an inescapable conclusion: YES.

9

Writing a Resume—and Getting an Interview

ॐ

Nothing else you write can make so big a difference in your life as your application for a job.

You should apply in *writing*. When you telephone for a job, you do it at *your* convenience. *You* choose the moment to call, and the chances of your potential employer being free to talk with you—or, more important, even being interested in doing so—are remote. If you want to be taken seriously, write.

What you write is a resume,* with a covering letter. Some of these will end up in a wastebasket, unread, but most businesses and organizations will respond to a well-written approach.

The point of the exercise is to secure an interview

---

* *Resume* can be *resumé* or *résumé*, depending on your dictionary. Since few typewriters have accent keys, and they can be a nuisance to activate on word processors, *resume* is common usage in business correspondence.

and possibly a job, and that objective should guide your thinking. Before you do any writing, think about what you have to offer and how those skills and experience can be presented in terms of what the job requires.

Don't be a pessimist and conclude right away that you don't have the qualifications. Most people have more than they realize, but an amazing number either can't pull them together in coherent form or are too lazy to think about how they relate to the person receiving the application.

Start by doing some research on the market.

- *What kinds of skills and experience are required?*

- *What can you do that demonstrates that you have made some effort to learn about the company or organization?*

- *What can you tell them about the contribution you're qualified to make?*

Research can also mean finding a person to help get you in the door. Russell Reynolds, the executive recruitment firm, estimates that 70 percent of jobs are landed through personal contacts.

Dear Charlie:

Attached is the resume of someone I think you should meet.

But you still need a resume. It is frequently the first detailed information a potential employer will receive about you. It is your first contact with a company, and will affect an interviewer's first impression of you.

How to write a resume

A resume summarizes the facts about you, your education, and your experience that are relevant to the job you want. It positions you in the mind of the reader.

Your purpose is to make it as easy as possible for a potential employer to decide whether you might be a candidate for the job at hand—and whether it is worthwhile to go to the next step of an interview. Remember: The purpose is an interview, not a place in a file drawer.

What should be put in, and in what order? What is best left out? What is the right style—telegraphic or full sentences, first person or third person? What is the appropriate format?

Here are some suggestions:

1. Stick to standard, conventional forms

A prospective employer, confronted by a pile of applications, will not be charmed by those that must be figured out like a puzzle. They waste time.

No fancy formats or pop-ups. A standard 8½-by-11-inch page, designed to go in a standard #10 business envelope, is the *only* professional style. It can be typed or set in type; just make it neat and not fussy. Avoid italics or special typefaces or colored paper.

Resumes on videotape are seldom acceptable except in companies where show biz is in style.

2. Keep it simple, keep it straight

A resume should be straightforward, logical—and truthful. Make it easy for the reader to understand you and to track your career.

And write it yourself. No professional consultant knows you as well as you do, nor cares as much about getting you a job.

3. Keep it short

Try to get it on one page, two at the most. If you have little experience, padding won't help.

If you have decades, it is all the more impressive to stick to highlights. If you can point to considerable accomplishments, put these on a separate paper—following the tight chronology of your jobs and responsibilities.

Don't forget that there will be a cover letter in which you can elaborate on any points of special relevance.

4. First things first

Name, address, phone number at the top.

Next, state a job objective—factually, without embellishment. A prospective employer doesn't care if you want a "challenging position." (Sometimes we think we would hire, sight unseen, anybody who would be willing to get out all that nonchallenging work every day.)

Some people are qualified to pursue alternative careers—in either law or finance, for example. In this event prepare two different resumes—one for each objective, with the balance of the resume tailored to that objective.

5. List jobs (including locations and dates)— starting with the most recent

An employer is more interested in what you have been doing lately than in what you did ten years ago. If you gained your most relevant experience some years ago on an earlier job, make it stand out by the amount of detail in the resume (and cover letter)—not by changing the order.

Include some definition of the *size* of the business you worked in (such as sales), unless the size will be obvious to all readers. Describe the scope of your responsibilities and, most important, *your* accomplishments. Be honest; if you were part of a team, say so. Don't exaggerate; make it believable.

If you've been out of work at some point in your career, or have worked for companies that no longer exist, you may be tempted to omit those experiences. Resist the temptation.

Fill in all the gaps; otherwise, it looks as though you're hiding something. For the period you've been out of work, simply say something like "1990–1991 Personal Projects," or whatever happens to be the truth.

6. Cover education and relevant outside interests

Include all degrees and dates. Leave out high school (unless you're applying for a first job or attended an unusual school).

Then list any boards of directors you serve on, and memberships in professional or trade associations. Next, membership in significant community or volunteer service organizations, with the most important ones first.

If you have published any articles or books, include these as well.

If you are fresh out of college or graduate school, extracurricular activities can be relevant.

7. Personal information

Briefly cover significant personal facts. *Briefly.* List all special skills, such as facility in a foreign language. You never know when such secondary abilities will be the deciding factor in getting you an interview, or even a job.

8. Edit

Start by putting in everything; then boil it down to a page or so by cutting the marginal points or ones that barely apply. If they don't directly make the case about your candidacy, take them out or cut them down. Stick to the facts, and be specific.

Be careful with abbreviations; people may not know what they mean. Give the full names of companies, trade associations, governmental bodies.

Take out all unnecessary words. Shorten everything to the extent of writing in telegraphic style—without verbs, articles or connectives. Write in the third person: "Managed 64-person department," not "I managed . . ."

Then test-market by showing it to someone who will bring a fresh perspective and who's capable of asking tough questions, like "Is this really what you wanted to say?" Then edit it again.

9. Make it perfect—make it professional

No typos. No misspellings. A small typo will detract from an otherwise stellar resume. It comes off as unprofessional and careless, and sends all the wrong signals.

You don't have to go to the expense of printing your resume, but get top-quality photocopies. Crisp and black, without smudges.

What to leave out

People put the strangest things in their resumes. The test of what to include is the same as it is for anything else you write: Is it relevant? Is it true?

Here are some items to downplay or drop:

- *Age or gender*—not essential, seldom relevant, and the law says you cannot be asked. But, of course, prospective employers will figure out whether you're male or female, and will get a pretty good idea of your age from the dates on your resume.
- *Honors or prizes*—unless they are genuinely important in your field.
- *Height and weight*—unless it is relevant to the requirements of the job.
- *Travel*—unless relevant.
- *References*—generally not necessary. The employer will check you out at the appropriate time, and the phrase "References furnished upon request" is gratuitous. EXCEPTION: if you're responding to a blind advertisement, with a box number, a list of references and telephone numbers is appropriate—to help the interviewer select candidates from a mass of unscreened responses.
- *Salary requirement*—if appropriate, put this in the cover letter.
- *Hobbies*—who cares?
- *Race or religion*—best left out. The law says you cannot be asked.
- *Clubs*—not necessary.
- *Photograph*—only beginners seem to include their pictures.

How to get your resume read

Never send a resume without a covering letter. It takes time to go through a resume. Employers decide from your covering letter whether your resume is worth that time—and ultimately warrants an interview.

The letter is your opportunity to stand out, to tell the reader how to think about you. The resume sells somewhat indirectly; the letter is a direct sale.

Here are some tips:

1. Think about the reader

What can you offer that will benefit a prospective employer? Do you have relevant experience, training, or education?

Consulting with a young law student, we were struck by his proposed letter applying for a job in the Environmental Protection Agency. Almost every paragraph started with "I," as it outlined his impressive credentials. A better letter started by stating:

> *According to press reports, your agency is under enormous pressure in staff and budgets, and it is obvious that you must have people who can move fast and carry a heavy load. Here are several reasons why my background should be helpful to EPA in these ways.*

Try to come up with a benefit to the organization that will accrue from your joining it.

2. Identify the sort of job you're looking for

State it clearly and at once. Say what led you to apply—a want ad, a recommendation from a friend, the reputation of the firm.

A letter applying for a job as a research analyst started in this mysterious way:

Dear Mr. Ball:

It's spring already—a time to think about planting seeds. Some seeds are small, like apple seeds. Others are bigger. Coconuts, for example. But big or little, a seed can grow or flourish if it's planted in proper soil.

The applicant would have done better to start like this:

Dear Mr. Ball:

I understand that you are looking for a research analyst.

Better straight to the point, however trite, than roundabout, however ingenious. Mr. Ball wants to know what the letter is *about;* he doesn't have time to play guessing games with his mail. Don't emulate the fellow who had his tonsils removed through his belly button, just to be different.

3. Pique the interest of the reader

You can do that without missing a beat.

Dear Ms. Smith:

According to the grapevine, you've been looking for an experienced research analyst for three months. If so, then it's strange that in such a small community we didn't know each other until now.

That is not the same as trying to attract favorable attention by buttering up a potential employer, which doesn't work:

Dear Ms. Smith:

I have long admired your firm as one of the most reputable and professional in the country. It is clear that your success cannot be attributed to accident or coincidence.

Flattery may still have its uses in business, but introducing yourself as a flatterer won't impress most employers.

Here are two openings that go straight to the point in interesting ways:

Dear Ms. Page:

Do you need an exceptionally fast accountant? If so, I may be your man.

Dear Mr. Kilgour:

Our mutual friend Charles Hartigan has urged me to write to you about your plan to create a publicity department. I would like to help you set it up—and I know how to do it, as you can see from my resume.

4. Address an individual, never a title by itself

Don't address your envelope ATTENTION—PERSONNEL DIRECTOR, or MANAGER or HEAD OF ACCOUNTING DEPARTMENT.

Raphaelson throws out applications addressed only to "Creative Director" on the ground that if the writer is too lazy to find out his name, he or she will be too lazy to do a good job.

Spell all names right. It is astonishing how often job applicants misspell names, including the names of the firms they want to work for. A message comes through even before the letter is read: "This applicant can't be seriously interested in working here."

Check and double check all names, even those you think you know. Are you sure it's "Field" and not "Fields"? How many "f's" are there in "Hefner"? Does Eliot spell his name with one "l" or two, one "t" or two? Is it "Ann" or "Anne"? "Ogilvie" or "Ogilvy"?

5. Be specific and factual

Once you've made clear what job you want, then touch on your chief qualification. Avoid egotistical abstractions such as:

> *Ambition mixed with striving for excellence is one of my strongest assets.*

Ask yourself how you would feel *saying* that to a prospective employer. If it would embarrass you in person, don't put it in writing.

So how do you indicate personal characteristics that may be among your most important qualifications? Be specific and factual. Offer evidence in support of any claim of ability, and put the claim as modestly as you can.

> *You'll see from my resume that I've been studying accounting and tax law at night for two years while working full-time as a bookkeeper for R. Smith. On weekends from January through April I help my uncle, a tax consultant, with his income tax business.*
>
> *I draw your attention to this as an indication of more than ordinary ambition to become a first-class accountant.*

Touch on your most important accomplishments in the same matter-of-fact style. Cover your pertinent responsibilities.

Never brag, but don't hesitate to cite authentic evidence of your value. If you don't blow your own horn, who will?

6. Be personal, direct, and natural

You are a human being writing to another human being. Neither of you is an institution. Be businesslike and courteous, but not stiff and impersonal.

The more your letter sounds like *you,* the more it

will stand apart from the letters of your competitors. But don't try to dazzle the reader with your sparkling personality. You wouldn't show off in an interview, so why show off in a letter? If you make each sentence sound the way you would say it across a desk, there will be plenty of personality in your letter.

7. Be brief

Keep your letter short. Most good covering letters make their point in about a half page; few run longer than a page. If your cover letter looks more formidable than your resume, you have defeated your purpose.

8. Propose a specific next step

You will be writing to a person or to a box number. In either case, close the letter with a clear and precise statement of how you wish to proceed toward an interview—remember that's your objective, not a "We'll keep your letter on file" response.

Avoid such mumblings as:

Hoping to hear from you soon.
Thank you for your time and consideration.
I'm looking forward to the opportunity of discussing a
    position with you.

All such conclusions place the burden of the next step on your busy prospective employer. Why make someone else work on your behalf? Do the job yourself.

I'll call your office Wednesday afternoon to see if you'd like me to come in for an interview.

I'm free for an interview every morning until 8:45, and Thursdays after 2:30. I'll call your office Tuesday after-

noon to find out if you'd like to get together at any of these times.

At this stage you *should* volunteer to telephone. A phone call now makes things easy for the person at the other end. If you don't call, then someone has to go to the trouble of calling or writing you.

If you are writing to a box number, you can't take the next step. But you can make the next step simple by enclosing a self-addressed stamped postcard that's easy to fill out:

_____ Please call my secretary for an appointment.

Name_____

Telephone_____

_____Sorry, you're not quite right for this job.

Or you could end your letter like this:

If you'd like me to come in for an interview, you can reach me at (999) 438-6688, extension 276, from 10 A.M. to 1 P.M., and from 2 P.M. to 6:30 P.M. on working days. I can arrange to get away for a couple of hours any day but Monday; best for me would be Thursday morning.

The idea is to make it as simple as you possibly can for your prospective employer to set up an appointment at a time that's convenient.

9. Send different letters to different readers

With the exception of the cases noted in our earlier discussion of the resume, you will probably want to send the same resume to all potential employers. But you may not want to approach all of them exactly the same way in your covering letter.

Certain of your qualifications may be more important to one employer than to another. Take the trouble to tailor your letter for each of them.

10. Send lots of letters

Finding the right job in the shortest time is in part a numbers game. Send your letter and resume to as many different people in an organization as you can; it is impossible to predict where the opportunities lie. And mail to lots of companies. The more people who see your resume, the greater the odds that one of them will have an open job and invite you to come in for an interview.

Send a second letter if you haven't had a response after a few weeks. It's possible that the addressee was traveling, that your application was mistakenly screened out and never seen, that it was forgotten, or that a job has opened up that wasn't there when you first wrote.

Write a follow-up letter

Follow up *all* interviews with a short note, confirming your interest and expressing appreciation for the opportunity to have met. Try to find something specific to comment on, something beyond a perfunctory "thank you."

Dear Ms. Oldham:

After I left your office, I realized that we'd talked for more than an hour. It was stimulating—and made the job seem most attractive.

You mentioned your need for someone who truly understands the consumer. I spent three years selling stoves door-to-door plus five years in a research firm. I figure that I've spent 5,000 hours talking person-to-person with some 3,000 consumers in 20 states.

I hope to be able to put this experience to work for you.

Whatever you say, don't gush or grovel. Don't exaggerate your appreciation for the interview or your interest in the job. Here, as in everything you write, candor and sincerity will serve you best. A good follow-up letter certifies your interest and in many cases will set you apart from your competitors.

If you don't get the job, don't give up—especially when you feel you've made a favorable impression. Find ways to stay in touch, in writing, with anybody who already thinks well of you.

A letter from time to time can make sure you come to mind in case a suitable job opens up, or in case your interviewer hears of one in another company. You might fire off an occasional clipping on some subject of mutual interest, accompanied by a brief note. You could report on some activity since the interview that's new and bears on the line of work you're looking for. Or you can simply reaffirm your interest.

There is no magic in all of this. If nothing works, maybe what you need is more relevant training, or experience at a lower level. A sign in a college placement office said:

YOUR RESUME IS FINE
(Change Your Life!)

KATHERINE RAPHAELSON   134 Charles St.
Boston, MA 02114
(617) 723-8896

OBJECTIVE: A job in marketing that involves writing, communications and people.

BUSINESS EXPERIENCE
BBN Software Products Corp. Cambridge, MA   **June, 1984 –Present**

Marketing Assistant for firm that develops, markets and sells engineering software.

Manage sales lead systems; write customer newsletter, press releases, marketing literature; manage direct mail projects; trade shows and seminars; technical demonstrations of products; market research projects.

Wellesley College Writing Program   **February– May, 1984**
Wellesley, MA

Taught writing and English grammar to two foreign Wellesley students; created and graded assignments.

Marie Case Communications Jackson, WY   **Summer 1982**

Part-time office help and writing for small advertising agency.

Chicago Sun Times Chicago, IL   **Summer 1981**

Part-time researcher, writer and assistant for syndicated columnist.

ACTIVITIES
Volunteer, Mass. General Pediatrics Intensive Care Unit
New England Masters Swimming

EDUCATION
Wellesley College. B.A. 1984 cum laude, English major
Trinity College, Dublin. Visiting student 1982–1983

SKILLS
Speak, read and write fluent French, some Spanish.
Proficiency in computers.

In 1987, this resume helped its subject get hired as a director of public relations for a successful small company.

10

Make It Look Easy to Read

ॐ

Neatness counts.

If what you've written looks formidable or messy or sloppy, your reader braces for an ordeal before reading a word. "This looks like heavy going" is the message you deliver, at first glance.

If what you've written looks easy to take in and get through, you're off to a good start.

Many word processing programs allow you to preview the appearance of an entire page. This feature can help you decide what improvements in looks may be called for. And the word processor's virtuosity in formatting makes it easy to put those improvements into effect.

Here are some ways to make everything you write look *professional*—inviting to read, easy to understand, and simple to refer to.

1. Start with a heading

Put it top center in capital letters. This orients your reader at once.

OFFICE CLOSES FRIDAY NOON

PURSE THIEF AT LARGE

2. Keep paragraphs short

Wherever you see a long paragraph, break it into two or more short ones.

3. Use typographic devices for clarity and emphasis

For extra emphasis, underline entire sentences. When underlining sentences or phrases, <u>use a single continuous underline</u> rather than a <u>choppy</u>-<u>looking underline</u>, <u>one</u> <u>word</u> <u>at</u> <u>a</u> <u>time</u>, which slows reading.

To stress key ideas, put them into indented paragraphs. This emphasizes them by setting them apart. Italics can add even greater emphasis.

Number your points. Numbered or lettered points look best when the numbers or letters are a couple of spaces to the left of the text margin, like the *a.* and *b.* that follow.

    a. Word processors put tools into your hands that used to be available only to printers. Boldface type, for example, can make it easy for your reader to scan your main points. (We use it for that purpose throughout this book.)

    b. "Hanging" your letters and numbers in the margin makes your divisions and subdivisions easier to follow.

4. Use upper and lower case

Never use all capitals except for headings. They are hard to read when they run on for more than a few words.

5. Break up large masses of type

Use subheads. Type them in capitals and lowercase, underline them or put them in boldface, and leave plenty of space above and below.

6. Use space to separate paragraphs

It looks neater than indents, in typewritten material.

Use single spacing between lines, double spacing between paragraphs. Drafts of documents for which you are soliciting comments should be triple-spaced throughout. It makes editing easier.

7. Handle numbers consistently

Newspapers generally spell out numbers for ten and under, and use numerals for 11 and up.

It is easier to grasp big numbers when you write $60 million rather than $60,000,000.

8. Make charts easy to handle—and interesting

If your document includes wide charts, don't make the reader turn it sideways to read them. Use horizontal foldouts.

Consider whether your charts need to be in the body of your document at all. Might they go at the end, as appendices? Your document will look less formidable if it is uninterrupted by graphs and charts.

Put them in color, if possible, particularly if they have to go in the body rather than in an appendix. Color adds vitality and variety.

Number your appendices and separate them clearly with tabs. This makes them easy to find.

9. Make it perfect

No typos, no strikeovers, no misspellings, no smudges. Nothing to distract the reader. Nothing to offend the eye.

Photocopy equipment should be adjusted to reproduce the sharpness of your original without smudges or dirty border marks. Poor photocopies look cheap and ugly, and discourage reading.

10. Number your pages, even in early drafts

If inserted material messes up the order, use 1A, 1B, and so on. Nothing is more annoying than trying to refer to an item in an unnumbered paper.

Before typing or printing your final draft, run your eye over it with these techniques in mind. What can you do to make it look more interesting? Where will your meaning be illuminated by subheadings, indents, underlines, enumeration?

Write for the eye as well as the mind.

Ogilvy & Mather Worldwide

Memorandum

Date September 7, 1982

From David Ogilvy

To Directors

If everybody in our company took an exam in writing, the highest marks would go to the 14 Directors. The better you write, the higher you go in Ogilvy & Mather. People who think well, write well. Woolly minded people write woolly memos, woolly letters and woolly speeches. Good writing is not a natural gift. You have to *learn* to write well.

Here are 10 hints: Read the Roman-Raphaelson book on writing. Read it three times. Write the way you talk. Naturally. Use short words, short sentences and short paragraphs. Never use jargon words like *reconceptualize, demassification, attitudinally, judgmentally*. They are hallmarks of a pretentious ass. Never write more than two pages on any subject. Check your quotations. Never send a letter or memo on the day you write it. Read it aloud the next morning -- and then edit it. If it is something important, get a colleague to improve it. Before you send your letter or your memo, make sure it is crystal clear what you want the recipient to do. If you want ACTION, *don't* write. Go and *tell* the guy what you want.

David

Hard to read. Hard to absorb.

Ogilvy & Mather Worldwide

Memorandum

Date   September 7, 1982

From   David Ogilvy

To   Directors

HOW TO WRITE

If everybody in our company took an exam in writing, the highest marks would go to the 14 Directors.

The better you write, the higher you go in Ogilvy & Mather. People who <u>think</u> well, <u>write</u> well.

Woolly minded people write woolly memos, woolly letters and woolly speeches.

Good writing is not a natural gift. You have to <u>learn</u> to write well. Here are 10 hints.

1. Read the Roman-Raphaelson book on writing. Read it three times.

2. Write the way you talk. Naturally.

3. Use short words, short sentences and short paragraphs.

4. Never use jargon words like *reconceptualize, demassification, attitudinally, judgmentally*. They are hallmarks of a pretentious ass.

5. Never write more than two pages on any subject.

6. Check your quotations.

7. Never send a letter or a memo on the day you write it. Read it aloud the next morning -- and then edit it.

8. If it is something important, get a colleague to improve it.

9. Before you send your letter or your memo, make sure it is crystal clear what you want the recipient to do.

10. If you want ACTION, <u>don't</u> write. Go and <u>tell</u> the guy what you want.

                                        David

The memo as sent—easy to read and absorb.

11

Edit Everything You Write

࡞

Never send out the first draft of anything important. Good writers consider editing an essential part of the writing process, not just a final perfectionist polishing. Edit your work:

- To shorten
- To sharpen and clarify
- To simplify
- To check for accuracy and precision
- To improve order and logic
- To make sure nothing is left out
- To review tone
- To examine everything from the reader's point of view

The first rule: If it isn't essential, cut it out. Go through your draft once asking only this question: *What can I get rid of?*

Cut unnecessary words, phrases, sentences, paragraphs. Mark Twain said that writers should strike out every third word on principle: "You have no idea what vigor it adds to style."

Go through your draft a second time with these questions in mind:

1. Are you mumbling?

In putting together a first draft, it speeds things up to get *something* on paper, even if it only approximates what you want to say. But never settle for an approximation in your final draft.

Have you chosen the verbs and adjectives that express your meaning precisely? Could you be less abstract and more down-to-earth? Scrutinize every important word.

2. Have you got things in the best order?

This point was originally number six instead of number two. In editing, we decided it was *second* in importance—and closely related to point three.

Good writers shift things around a lot. This used to be a laborious business calling for scissors and Scotch tape and a lot of patience. With word processing you can take your work apart and reassemble it in seconds.

Many good writers print out a hard copy of each draft, to make it easy to compare the revised version against the original. It is not unusual to decide that some of your shifts of order aren't improvements after all.

3. Are there any holes in your argument?

Put yourself in your reader's shoes. Does everything follow logically?

Don't expect your reader to leap from point to point like a goat on a rocky hillside. Make sure your trail is clear, smooth, and well marked.

4. Are your facts right?

Check all statistics and statements of fact. A single bad error can undermine your reader's confidence in your paper.

In particular, check quotations. "I quote a lot," says an erudite author. "I always check, even when I am in no doubt. And I am *always* wrong."

5. Is the tone right?

Too stiff? Too chummy? Lacking in sympathy? Rude? Again put yourself in your reader's place and change anything that you, as a reader, might find offensive.

An example of editing

Here are five instances, taken from a single paper, of how editing shortened, sharpened, and clarified what the writer was trying to say:

First draft	Second draft
Consumer perception of the brand changed very positively.	The opinion of consumers improved.
Generate promotion interest through high levels of advertising spending.	Advertise heavily to build interest in promotions.

Move from product advertising to an educational campaign, one that would instruct viewers on such things as . . .	Move from product advertising to an educational campaign on subjects like . . .
Using the resources of our organization in Europe, in addition to our Chicago office, we have been able to provide management with alternatives they had previously been unaware of.	Our offices in Europe and Chicago produced alternatives that management hadn't known about.
Based on their small budget, we have developed a media plan which is based on efficiency in reaching the target audience.	We developed a media plan that increases the efficiency of their small budget by focusing on prospects.

Two secrets of editing

No matter how good an editor you are already, you will become better if you follow these practices:

- *Let time elapse between drafts.*

- *Solicit the opinion of other people.*

Have a clean copy of your draft printed out or typed. Set it aside. Get away from it at least overnight. Then come back to it in the morning.

You'll see it with new eyes. Imperfections that were invisible the day before will now pop out at you. Through some alchemy of time, you'll know what to do about them.

When you ask for comments from other people— colleagues, friends, anybody whose opinion you respect—you're putting them to work for you. If somebody's suggestions are helpful, say "Thank you" and use them. If you disagree with them, say "Thank you" and don't use them.

No need to argue or prove your consultant wrong. It's your work and you are making the decisions. You'll find that nearly everybody will spot something you overlooked. It can be invaluable just to discover that a point isn't clear.

David Ogilvy sends drafts of all important papers to several of his associates with the handwritten injunction: *Please Improve*. He has been the beneficiary of so many improvements that he now lives in a 60-room castle in France.

NEW EXAMPLES

~~If~~ *annual reports of U.S. corporation typify* ~~there is any kind of business report that everybody~~ *what most people*
~~thinks~~ of as ~~turgid, bureaucratic, impersonal,~~ *impenetrable business writing.* ~~and~~
~~unreadable, it is the annual report of U.S.~~
~~corporations.~~ *And* ~~Most~~ people accept that ~~it is~~ *such a style is in* the nature
of *these* ~~such~~ reports, that nothing can be done to make them
more readable.

Most people — but not Warren Buffett, Chairman of ~~But not everyone. One of the most admired is the~~
Berkshire Hathaway ~~report, written by its Chairman,~~
~~Warren Buffett, who also happens to be~~ *and* one of the
richest men in America. ~~His 1989 report stressed the~~
~~reason for favoring longterm investment commitments~~
~~rather than moving frequently from one investment to~~
~~another.~~

> "We have found splendid business relationships to
> be so rare and so enjoyable that we want to retain
> all we develop. This decision is particularly
> easy for us because we feel that these
> relationships will produce good -- though perhaps
> not optimal -- financial results."

We wish that all *[business writing papers]* ~~reports of all kinds~~ could be
written more like Buffett's annual reports.
Here are ~~some typical~~ excerpts from
one of them.

Editing improved even the improvements in this new edition.

143

12

Finding the Time to Write Well

❧

Writing better does not mean writing *more*. There is paper enough in our lives now, and precious little time to read it.

This book has suggested some of the ways that improving your writing can save time for other people. But what about *your* time? While you respect the time of others, you must also protect your own.

It takes time to write well. Peter Drucker, the respected authority on business practices, cautions us against assuming there are twenty-four hours in a day—or even eight hours. He estimates that in a typical workday there are perhaps one or two hours that you can use productively. The difference between *busy* executives and *effective* ones is how they use that time.

Look for time-savers to help you cope with the

paper you receive and respond to in writing. The level of paper rises as you do. It takes skill to dispatch it.

Try to handle paper only once. Decide quickly whether to answer it, file it, or toss it in the wastebasket. The biggest time waster is shuffling things from one pile to another while you drown in a sea of indecision.

Respond to easy matters instantly. Write your comments directly on letters and memos, and return them *at once.* Or send short handwritten notes of direction, praise, or criticism.

Save dictation for more formal responses or brief ones—a half page or less. Anything longer requires more organization and less verbosity than most people can achieve while dictating.

There is no rule that says you must answer (or file) everything that is sent to you. If in doubt, toss it out.

Some papers require study. Read them actively. Get to the principal arguments, and decide what must be done.

Consider a "maturing file" for knotty problems. Many disappear if given time. Others call for more thought.

All this will help you clear the decks—at the office or at home—for the more important parts of your job. High among them will be the major papers you write.

Afterword

Other Books That Will Help You Write Better

Most people who write well read a lot. They read many kinds of good writing, past and current—good fiction, good essays, good history, good journalism.

If you want to write better, read Mark Twain and Hemingway. Read the best of today's columnists, among them Mary McGrory, William Safire, Mike Royko, and George Will. For consistently lively reporting, read *The Economist.* You'll get the shapes and rhythms of good writing into your head.

Reading good writing will help you more than reading *about* good writing—and it's a lot more fun. But there are books on writing, and some reference books, that you may find helpful. Among the best:

The Elements of Style, *William Strunk, Jr., and E. B. White, Macmillan (81 pages).* No other book has helped so many writers, professional and non-professional, avoid the cliché and the vulgarism and find their own voices. Concise and elegant.

Managing Correspondence—Plain Letters, *a Records Management Handbook published by the federal government and available from the Superintendent of Documents, Washington, D.C. 20402 (53 pages).* An excellent manual by an anonymous government author. Contains a "watchlist" of overworked and misused words—and a useful set of questions to ask about any letter or memorandum.

Webster's New Collegiate Dictionary, *G. & C. Merriam Co.* One of the few reference works that draws distinctions between many near-synonyms, clearly explaining subtle differences of meaning.

American Heritage Dictionary, *Houghton-Mifflin.* A unique "usage panel" reports on what constitutes good contemporary usage of hundreds of words and expressions. (Also draws distinctions between near-synonyms.)

On Writing Well, (Fourth Edition), *William Zinsser, HarperCollins (288 pages).* More for the professional writer of nonfiction than for the business writer. But enlightening, entertaining, and wise—well worth reading if you get hooked on improving your writing.

Successful Direct Marketing Methods, *Bob Stone, Crain Books (334 pages).* In the opinion of many professionals, this is the most complete and authoritative book on direct marketing. It covers every aspect of selling through the mail.

Strictly Speaking, *Edwin Newman, Bobbs-Merrill (224 pages).* The best attack on jargon, clichés, and errors.

Language in Thought and Action, *S. I. Hayakawa, Harcourt Brace Jovanovich (307 pages).* The basic book on semantics, a study of the relationship between language and behavior. A stimulating guide to accurate thinking, reading, listening, and writing.

Watch Your Language, *Theodore M. Bernstein, Atheneum (276 pages).* The former assistant managing editor of *The New York Times* has put together, in dictionary form, his commonsense thoughts on hundreds of questions about usage that come up regularly. Authoritative but in no way pedantic.

Never Be Nervous Again, *Dorothy Sarnoff, with Gaylen Moore, Crown (212 pages).* A renowned speech consultant covers every element of the public presentation, from writing it to preparing its delivery to the delivery itself.

I Can See You Naked—A Fearless Guide to Making Great Presentations, *Ron Hoff, Andrews and McMeel (255 pages).* Dozens of meaty tips on how to be at your persuasive best when you're on your feet in the conference room.

Designer's Guide to Creating Charts & Diagrams, *Nigel Holmes, Watson-Guptill Publications (192 pages).* The graphics director of *Time* magazine serves up lucid advice on how to add both clarity and drama to visual aids. Illustrated by dozens of highly imaginative examples.

You Are the Message, *Roger Ailes with Jon Kraushar, Doubleday (178 pages).* Adviser to U.S. Presidents, top business executives, and celebrities, Ailes passes on valuable secrets he's learned about public speaking and communications. Practical advice leavened with anecdotes and examples.

***The Economist* Style Guide** *(141 pages).* Lively and witty advice on writing, based on this much-admired journal's own style manual and including such worthy principles as these:

The first requirement of The Economist *is that it should be readily understandable. Clarity of writing usually follows clarity of thought. So think what you want to say, then say it as simply as possible.*

- *Use the language of everyday speech, not that of spokesmen, lawyers or bureaucrats.*
- *Do not be hectoring or arrogant. Those who disagree with you are not necessarily stupid or insane. Nobody needs to be described as silly: let your analysis prove that he is.*
- *Don't boast of your own cleverness by telling readers that you correctly predicted something or that you have a scoop. You are more likely to bore or irritate than to impress them. . . .*

The editors understand the *purpose* of effective writing as well as its ingredients: "On only two scores can *The Economist* hope to outdo its rivals consistently. One is the quality of its analysis. The other is the quality of its writing."

&

About the Authors

Kenneth Roman and Joel Raphaelson worked together at Ogilvy & Mather Worldwide, a major advertising agency noted for its interest in good writing.

Mr. Roman is the former Chairman and Chief Executive. He is also the coauthor of *How to Advertise*.

Mr. Raphaelson is Senior Vice President, International Creative Services, and a frequent lecturer on writing and other subjects.

They thank David Ogilvy, who taught them a thing or two about good writing—and Tom Aydelotte, Hob Brown, Bill Bryan, Len Clark, John Groman, Jon Kraushaar, Manny Martinez, Kent Mitchel, and Stan Winston, for their many contributions to this Second Edition.